T0208556

Living a Meaningful Life Without Purpose

GERSHON WINKLER

BALBOA.
PRESS

A DIVISION OF HAY HOUSE

Balboa Press books may be ordered through booksellers or by contacting:

Balboa Press
A Division of Hay House
1663 Liberty Drive
Bloomington, IN 47403
www.balboapress.com
1 (877) 407-4847

Print information available on the last page.

ISBN: 978-1-9822-0610-9 (sc)
ISBN: 978-1-9822-0611-6 (e)

Balboa Press rev. date: 06/12/2018

"Our existence is not in vain. Its meaning may not be explicable to us, yet even when we do not know *what* it is, we know *that* it is."

- Abraham Joshua Heschel in *Moral Grandeur and Spiritual Audacity*, p. 11

To my sweet, amazing, insightful, beloved life-partner and best friend, Rabbi Dr. Miriam Ashina Maron, for ever so lovingly guiding me along the path of mindfulness with patience, humor, and wisdom.

Contents

Chapter One

IN THE GARDEN OF PARADOX

"The darkness of potentiality is the hotbed of anxiety. There is always more than one path to go, and we are forced to be free – we are free against our will – and have the audacity to choose, rarely knowing how or why."[1]

Ever have those moments when you feel like you're on a journey to *some*where, but you can't seem to get there. And the closer you think you're getting, the farther it turns out that you are. And no sooner do you think you're there, when you discover that you're not. Moreover, you have no clue what or where that somewhere *is*, nor do you have a clue of how to *get* there!?

And people are knocking on your door, offering to help you find truths you've never lost. And bestsellers like *this* one compete for your attention, promising to answer questions you never pondered and offer solutions to problems you never had. And videos flash before your

---

[1] A.J. Heschel in *Man is Not Alone*, p. 209

weary leery eyes claiming to reveal secrets to successes enjoyed mostly by those who succeeded in marketing them. And all around you, religions compete for your allegiance, quoting from the very same prophets who railed **against** religion. And visionaries are busily reaching for the future to cover up their failure to fathom the past or grasp the present. And researchers are promising remedies for ailments that elude them. And politicians are engaged in verbal Ponzi schemes founded upon votes naively invested by gullible constituents. And excitement abounds everywhere with the prospect that the end is near when we've barely begun.

And the world is turning and churning and you are getting dizzier and dizzier as the spin of technological progress continues its ever-accelerating spiral, whittling away at your organic nature and slowly transforming you into a mechanical operator of ever-shrinking keypads and a mesmerized worshiper of screens illuminated by light-emitting diodes and hopelessly addicted to hand-held rectangular portals to worldwide expanses of anything and everything while you sit there feeling useless in the back seat of your self-driven car.

And in the scheme of it all stand you so small, watching in puzzlement as life whirls around you while you remain abandoned on the outside looking in. And you wonder, how you wonder: "Where do *I* fit in? What is my purpose in *being*? What is the meaning of life, if there *is* one?" And the answers blowing in the wind, while they appear promising at first, only dissipate before your eyes like a passing mist.

For perhaps there **are** no answers. Because all of your

questions – every single one of them – is predicated upon assumptions you yourself have invented or adopted from others no less confounded than you. And so, round and round you go, burning tons of energy in your mad dash along the treadmill of life, running miles and miles toward an ever-elusive horizon, yet getting nowhere beyond where you've always been.

Or, in the words of the proverbial first couple – Adam and Eve: "I suddenly became aware that I am clueless, that I don't know why I'm here and what I'm supposed to be **doing** with my life!"

And Creator said to them: "Why all of a sudden has it become so urgent for you to have to know why you're here and what it is you're supposed to be doing with your life when it never concerned you *before*!? Did you perchance leaf through that forbidden book I warned you about? Namely, '*The Idiot's Guide to Good and Evil*'"?[2]

You see, the issues that disturbed Adam and Eve in their story are the very same issues that you and I are strapped with on our journey along the path laid-out before us. They don't begin to disconcert us until we arrive at the crossroads in the center of the Garden of Paradox, where stand the Tree of Life and the Tree of Knowledge of This and That and the Other – when we have crossed the threshold into adulthood, when we realize, as King David put it some 3,000 years ago: "For my mom and dad have kicked me out of the apartment, so I sure as hell hope there really *is* a Higher Power out there who will step in and take over."[3]

---

[2] Genesis 3:10-11

[3] Psalms 27:10

At home with our parents we felt safe and tended to, and hadn't yet encountered the big questions regarding life and purpose because mom and dad were sitting in the driver's seat and we were cozily playing in the back seat looking out the window at the passing scenery of a world we took for granted. And no less than was the purpose of life for a dog the continuous act of chasing a ball, the purpose of life for us was the continuous act of...um... chasing a ball. But when we eventually left the nest to find our own, the rules shifted, and so did we. We wondered why the car had stopped. And then we peered over the headrest of the seat in front of us only to realize there was no one at the helm, that it was up to us to climb into the front seat and grab hold of the steering wheel. Because the vehicle of our journey was idling at the crossroads, at the center of which stood a huge sign with two arrows, one pointing **this** way, one pointing **that** way; one reading "This way to the Tree of Living," and the other reading "This way to the Tree of Knowing."

Well, since we didn't know which road to take, it made sense that we would head to the Tree of Knowing, so that we can – you know – *know*! And so, we hurried down that road, driven by 8-cylinder urgency, by this overwhelming need to figure it out, to make sense out of life. And in our desperation, as soon as we arrived at the Tree of Knowing, we hungrily plucked its promising fruit and gulped it down without reading the ingredients and in total disregard of the warning label. To our surprise, the fruit of Knowing only made us more aware of how much we *didn't* know, of how much we were missing, of how naked we truly were. And we discovered, much to our disappointment, that instead of helping us to *know*, the fruit of the Tree of Knowing only confounded us further and we ended up more confused and befuddled than we were before. And the only knowing we came away with was knowing more clearly how clearly we didn't **know**!

The ancient masters spoke often of the concept of "revealing a handbreadth and concealing a handbreadth."[4] What this means is that every phase of revelation leads to further concealment; the more we know, the more it becomes apparent that we do *not* know. The more knowledge we uncover, the more we realize how *little* we've uncovered. "The closer you get," taught the 18th-century Nachmon of Breslav, "the farther away you really are."[5]

You know, the *Garden of Eden* story always bugged me. I mean, if we weren't meant to eat of the Tree of Knowledge of Good and Evil, why put it there to begin with? (Is this where the idea of "entrapment" came from?) The ancients explained it this way: Actually, the so-called Forbidden Fruit was **indeed** intended for consumption, only there was an important prerequisite. "The fruit of the Tree of Knowledge of Good and Evil," they taught, "was intended to be eaten, but only in combination with the fruit of all the **other** trees in the Garden. The prohibition was in regard to eating of the Tree of Knowledge alone, to the **exclusion** of the fruit from the other trees." Knowledge by itself, in other words, is deceptive. Abraham Joshua

---

[4] *Talmud Bav'li, Nedarim* 20b
[5] *Likutei MoHaRaN*, No. 63, para. 3

Heschel put it quite succinctly when he once described knowledge as "a pretext for higher ignorance."[6]

"The Serpent," taught the ancients, brought down the house specifically "through Wisdom," through the seductive allure of knowledge alone, absent any other ingredient.[7] It's sort of like how some doctors suggest that we not eat Sushi by itself since it's raw and uncooked, and that it's safer when you have it along with some *Wasabi* and *Sake*.

Living off of knowledge alone without incorporating all the **other** goodies, severs us from life and perpetuity; stunts our potential for endless growth and expansion; and clouds our vision of possibility. When it comes to knowledge, you have to cook it with at least one other ingredient, even if it's a grain of salt. By itself, it obscures.

The seduction was then very much the allure of bartering the inconvenience of Choice for the expediency of Knowledge. Because if you **know**, then you don't have to **choose**. So, the way out of the cumbersome dilemma of Choice, the Serpent suggested, is to partake of the Fruit of the Tree of **Knowledge**! With knowledge, he assured us, you will not need to deal with ever having to choose.[8]

It is important to understand the meaning of the Tree of Knowledge of Good and Evil and its badly-maligned fruit. The Knowing it wielded was not about the definitions or deeper meanings of Good and Evil but about clarity in regard to the **distinction** between the two that was "as clear as one distinguishes between sweet and bitter."[9] In

[6] *Man is Not Alone*, p. 150
[7] Zohar, Vol. 1, folio 35b
[8] *Tzeed'kat Ha'Tzadik*, No. 40
[9] Zohar, Vol. 1, folio 35a

reality, the Tree of Knowledge was Good – **period** – as was befitting for such a tree in the Garden of Eden, the Garden of All-Good. The problem, however, is that once the notion of "Good" was introduced, there inevitably also arose -- by default -- the notion of "Evil."[10] Just as the idea of hot automatically and instantaneously introduces the idea of cold, or as the idea of small implies the idea of big, or the idea of light implies that of dark. It would then be more accurate to interpret the name of this controversial tree as "The Tree of Knowledge of Good, and **therefore** *also* of Evil."

Adam and Eve did not realize that if they ingested the concept of Good, they would inevitably ingest along with it that of Evil, which would in turn blur or outright distort the purity of the quality of Good they presumed to have attained. And so, to this day, we have been grappling with discerning the Good from the Bad, since each is intertwined with the other.[11] It's kind of like a 14KT knotted gold necklace. It is still 14KT, but it is helplessly tangled.

Eating of the Tree of Knowledge exclusive of the other trees altered our minds to the effect that, instead of coming away with **clarity** around the distinctions between right and wrong, we came away with **confusion** around both. We came away not with a Knowing but with a **presumption** of Knowing; we came away not knowing whether or not we knew. Thus, the more we **presume** to know, the more susceptible we become to bullshit. Or,

---

[10] *Sefer Yetzirah* 6:4; *Shelah HaKadosh, Torah Sh'be'ch'tahv, Ohr Chadash*, folio 270b; *Likutei MoHaRaN* 51:3

[11] Zohar, Vol. 2, folios 69a-b and Vol. 3, folio 80b

in the more eloquent words of the ancient masters: "As soon as the infant achieves any semblance of knowing and understanding, we begin to distance ourselves from its stool."[12] In other words, it doesn't smell too bad when you're changing diapers for a newborn, but as the months go by and baby learns, and begins to assume that it "knows," changing diapers becomes an increasingly unpleasant experience. Why do you suppose people who differ with you sometimes tell you that you are "**full** of it"? It's not that your learning and wisdom have no value, but – to quote the 16th-century Isaac Luria -- "What you read of what I wrote may not be what I meant when I wrote it." In other words, much of what we learn, we learn from within the narrows of our own personal *Gestalt*, absent the broader context of everything else around us. It's like calling applesauce a fruit salad, even though it's blended with nothing other than itself. Or boasting about how you're for Freedom of Speech while picketing the arrival of a speaker with an opinion different than yours.

Thus, the actual and **intended** Knowledge of Good and Evil is, again, about the crystal-clear **disambiguation** of one from the other in a scenario wherein the lines between both would otherwise be blurred. But eating of its fruit outside the context of the **rest** of the orchard resulted in a consciousness of ambiguity and uncertainty which in turn led to a distortion of *which* is *which* and *when*. In our attempt to free ourselves of Choice by eating of the Tree of Knowledge, we ended up with a scenario inundated with more Choice to deal with than **before** we got bamboozled into eating of it.

---

[12] *Talmud Bav'li, Sukah* 42b

Ever hear the story about the young blacksmith who apprenticed with an elder blacksmith for several years until he found out that the king was looking for one? Eager to make it on his own, the young apprentice thanks the elder for all that he'd taught him and gives him notice. The elder pleads with the young fella to please remain just a tad longer, that he's not really ready to make it on his own. But, to the elder's disappointment, the young apprentice leaves anyway and heads off to the palace, gets the interview, and lands the job. And they furnish him with everything he needs, some iron, an anvil, a couple of solid hammers, some hefty tongs, a late-model furnace, an apron -- the works. But to his dismay, as he is about to begin applying his skills, he realizes he'd never mastered the art of...*um*...kindling a **spark**!

And that's what happened in the Garden. We ate of the Tree of Knowledge before we'd even learned to kindle a spark, to create the necessary wherewithal by which the knowledge could flourish. And so, it wilted. And God took immediate action by gently ushering us out of the Garden lest we "partake of the Tree of Life and live forever"[13] as rookie blacksmiths loaded with tools and no spark.

On the Sunday after my Bar-Mitzvah ceremony, my parents asked me what I wanted as a birthday gift. I asked for a chemistry set. I'd seen one displayed in the window of Linick's Toy Store on Bay Parkway. And it looked really neat. Like, test tubes, jars of colorful chemical elements, a test-tube stand, even a microscope. I knew nothing about chemistry. Zilch. I didn't even know what the **word** meant. But I liked what the set **looked** like. "It was alluring

---

[13] Genesis 3:22

to the eyes, and promised to impart Wisdom."[14] Since they'd long ago given up on trying to understand me, my parents just rolled their eyes, shrugged, heaved a parental sigh, and got it for me. Within the first hour, I ended up breaking one of the test tubes trying to jam it into the test-tube stand, severely cutting my finger on the broken glass, and in the second hour I drove everyone out of the house due to the unbearable stench fuming from the chemically-incompatible blend I'd created, a mix of unidentifiable compounds that flew off the Periodic Table.

This is exactly what happened in the Garden of Eden.

Needless to say, I never played with a chemistry set ever again and failed the subject abysmally in high school. However, I **did** ask for a *biology* set when I turned 14, but that barely lasted half an hour before the stench of the thamaldihide-marinated amphibious cadaver drove my mother out of the house and into the street. When my father came home that night, he took me aside and gently encouraged me to stick to the Talmud, which I've safely done ever since.

Outside the Garden, which is where you and I live, we have of Knowledge only what we **presume** to know, but in essence we're all about **Choice**. We are always having to **choose** what it is we think we **might** know, but deep down we admittedly **don't**. We make what we conveniently refer to as "an *informed* choice." And that choice becomes more or less a sort of kind of neo-pseudo Knowing which – due to its artificial composition – may or may not last as such, and at times, or **with** time, might very well collapse into what we call "an erroneous assumption" or an "error in

---

[14] Genesis 3:6

judgment," or "hindsight." What you think you know is then basically a gamble. Our world is designed this way. It's like Tiffany's. There is every possibility to choose from, depending on your budget and on how fast you can get your shopping done before closing time without maxing your credit card.

The only true remnants of Knowing outside the Garden are the so-called Laws of the Universe. Physics is a Knowing. But what **you** know about Physics is a Choice. Otherwise, you wouldn't have 233 different theories on any given theme of Physics to...*um*...**choose** from. Gravity is an absolute, not what you think you **know** about Gravity, but Gravity it**self**. What you think you **know** about Gravity can be easily disputed by other people who think **they** know about it, which means that the rest of us need to choose which *un*-Knowing we should adopt. Abraham Joshua Heschel said it best: "There is only one truth, but there are many ways of misunderstanding it."[15] Ever since I read those words, I stopped asking people what religion they are or what political side of the aisle they're on. Instead, I ask them "Which misunderstanding of the 'only one truth' do **you** believe in?"

Knowing is something that supersedes you and overrides any choice you'd wish to make during its process. *Peeing* is a Knowing. So is a seizure or a spasmic coughing fit, or falling off a cliff. None of these leave us any space for Choice. You cannot choose to not.

The common denominator of all Knowing, whether Gravity or Cavity, is that they may play a role in the drama of your existence, but your existence plays no role in *their*

---

[15] *Man is Not Alone*, p. 204

drama. They are the unalterable templates of the cosmos as established by the ineffable mystery behind all that is, was and will be. So, when they asked the second-century Akiva whether everything is predetermined or whether we have free choice, his response was: "Everything is indeed pre-determined, and the choice is **yours**."[16] In other words, *your* story, that is, the one **you** create as your life unfolds, is a Reality of **Choice** operating within the spokes of the Wheel of **Knowing** as it spins across the pathway of **Time**.

In creating your unique story by the choices which you make in the unfolding of your life, you embark upon the journey to what so many antediluvian cultures referred to as the "Tree of Life." The role of the obstacles stationed along the pathways of our journey[17] is not so much to *prevent* us from finding the answers we seek as it is to *enable* us to do so,[18] possible only if we approach with the knowing that we don't. When we let go of the destination we stand a far better chance of getting there. And in the end, we will probably discover that we've been standing there all along.[19]

So, if we're only here because the Great Mystery *put* us here, then what meaning is there in purpose and what purpose is there in meaning? And although that is precisely how we start out, being placed here whether we want to or not, the task is to evolve to where we no longer *happen* to be but *choose* to be.[20]

---

[16] *Mishnah, Avot* 3:19

[17] Genesis 3:24

[18] 18th-century Rabbi Shimshon Raphael Hirsch on Genesis 3:24

[19] Exodus 3:5

[20] Deuteronomy 30:19

It is for this reason that any attempt by Adam and Eve to bee-line it to the "Tree in the middle of the Garden" a *second* time -- in the hope of coming to it as Tree of *Life* – was out of the question. Of *course* one wishes a second opportunity after realizing the failure of the first. But change of *mind* is not the same as change of *heart*. Hurting your partner's feelings and then changing your tune because of the uncomfortable nature of the consequence does not make for finer music. You need to first leave the Garden and work "by the sweat of your brow"[21] to make some actual shifts not only in mind, but in heart and soul as well. Only then might you be able to make your way past the discriminating Cherubim and the Flaming Sword of Contrariness back to the same Tree, albeit in its role as the Tree of *Life*.[22] Because, actually, the Tree of Living and the Tree of Knowing are one and the same tree. Which of its faces it mirrors to you is dependent upon which of **your** faces you choose to show **it**.

How appropriate, then, was the decision to close-off the road to the Tree of Life. The intent was to bar us from the danger, not the benefit, of making our way back to the "tree in the middle of the garden" while the taste of the Forbidden Fruit still lingered on our tongues. If we come to the Tree of Life in search of purpose, we come instead to the Tree of **Knowledge** all over again, because we are then not *choosing* to live but rather seeking a *reason* to live. In *choosing* to live, on the other hand, I am partnering my choice to exist with Creator's choice *that* I exist, and then

---

[21] Genesis 3:19
[22] Genesis 3:24

the Creator and I "dream the same dream in the same night."[23]

And so, the story goes, Cherubic spirits were assigned to the entrance of the pathway to the Tree of Life, to that very quality of the "tree in the middle of the garden" about which all of future humanity would obsess and toward which they would incessantly clamor -- to make sure that if we *do* make the effort, we will have the proper "passport," the intention of living life not merely as a *given* but also as a *receiving*, not merely as a *must* but as a *choice*.

> Looking at our own existence, we are forced to admit that the essence of existence is not in our will to live; we **must** live, and in living we obey. Existence is a compliance, not a desire; an agreement, not an impulse. In being we obey...It is only subsequently that we get to *will* what we *must*.[24]

Some two hundred years ago deep into the Carpathian Mountains of Russia, there lived a great master. He was known as Dov Bear. One day, a poor man from a nearby village came to the home of Dov Bear. He had a problem. His mom was seriously ill and he had no means of traveling across the Russian border to visit her. He had food for the journey, ample clothing to stay warm, a pair of reasonably good boots, but he was unable to afford payment of the fee

---

[23] *Tikunei Zohar,* folio 129b, based on Genesis 41:11
[24] A.J. Heschel in *Man is not Alone,* p. 203

required for the necessary travel documents. Dov Bear felt very sorry for the man and explained that he was clear out of funds, having just given away his last coin to an impoverished bride-to-be so that she could get married.

"What am I to do, Master!?" the man pleaded. Dov Bear pondered the situation for what seemed to be a long period of time. Then he got out of his chair, told the man not to worry, and disappeared into his study, shutting the door behind him.

The poor man sat down to wait when he heard the sound of crying, then wailing, and it grew increasingly intense with each moment. He got up and pressed his ear against the wall of Dov Bear's study and recoiled in shock when he realized that it was the master himself who was crying! Nervous and confused, the man sat back down again and waited, wondering and wondering and wondering what the master was sobbing about in there.

Finally, the door to the study opened and the master appeared, his bearded face stained with tears, his eyes blood-red from the intense crying. In his hands were several soggy sheets of paper, drenched with his tears.

"Here," said Dov Bear, handing the papers to the man. "Here are your travel documents. They will get you to your destination and back without any obstacles."

Puzzled and hesitant, the man took the wet papers from Dov Bear's hands and then looked to see what was written on them.

Nothing. They were totally blank and soaked through and through with tear drops.

"This?" he asked in a near-whisper. "This is my passport?"

"Absolutely," replied the master, removing a kerchief from his robe pocket and blowing his nose.

The man quickly thanked the old master and hurriedly bee-lined it out the door, totally convinced that Dov Bear must have lost it. But once outside, he noticed the long long long line of people of all ages and sizes waiting for their turn to consult with the sage regarding their life struggles. How, he wondered, how could Dov Bear be not right in his mind if so many people are still flocking to see him? Maybe there **is** something to these blank tear-drenched papers after all.

With faith in his heart, and just as much doubt, not to mention hesitation, the man slung his provisions over his shoulders and set out on his journey.

Hours later, he arrived at the border. He grew very nervous. "What am I thinking?" he asked himself, looking down at the blank papers which, during all this time, had still not dried-up. "No doubt the border guards are going to mock me, beat me, and send me back home."

Suddenly, a border guard approached. "Let me see your papers," he said, gruffly. The poor man handed the guard the blank papers still soaked with the tears of Dov Bear, then closed his eyes and held his breath. This is ridiculous, he thought to himself. I ought to just turn around and vamoose out of here. He slowly opened one eye and grimaced as he watched the fierce-looking guard leaf through the blank, tear-drenched papers. And then he shut his eyes again and readied himself for the blows.

"Good God, man!" shouted the guard. "Why didn't you **say** so?"

The poor man opened his eyes in bewilderment. "*Wha…?*"

"Of **course**, sir," the guard continued, "please resume your journey and cross the border, by all means, and I deeply apologize for being so rough with you. And if there is anything I can provide you for your journey, please do not hesitate to ask."

The guard then bowed to the poor man, as if he were the Czar himself, and gave him back the tear-drenched blank papers, clicked his heels, and sent him on his way across the border. To make a long story short, wherever he went, and to whomever he showed his soggy "travel papers," he was greeted like royalty and duly provided for in every which way until he had completed his journey and arrived at his destination.

On our life journey, you see, we carry suitcases loaded to the hilt with expectations. Most of these expectations are predicated upon our own home-brewn assumptions. When we seek support for something we are dealing with, or when we pray, or when we seek healing of any kind, we expect specific results in preconceived shapes and forms that are – again -- based on our presumptuously envisioned outcomes.

The man in the story expected official documentation with specific wording that would authorize his journey across the border. He expected a document infused with a definitive purpose. Instead, he got two sheets of blank papers drenched in tears; absent of purposefulness but soaked in meaningfulness. It made no sense to him, and he could not for the life of him understand how or why this would in any way serve the objective for which he had come, or any point at all. He could not for the life of him wrap his mind around how these blank soggy pages would in any shape or form address his cut-and-dry need.

But they did. And he learned that the way in which the healing or support we need comes to us is not necessarily congruent with our assumptions or expectations, and that when we let go of them and open ourselves up to what it is we receive, then it matters not whether what we get fits or doesn't fit our expectations, because often it is our expectations that have been part of the hurdle all along.

Every person, taught Abraham Joshua Heschel, is "valued by how many times he was able to see the world from a new perspective."[25] The first two of the proverbial Ten Commandments are about the arrogance of presuming we can put a face on God, on the meaning and purpose behind the mystery of existence, let alone assign it a particular definition or visage. What frightens me when I look deeply into the mystery is the realization that the object of my search appears closer than it really is. In essence, however, that which hovers directly in front of my nose is actually light years out of the reach of my grasp. But only when I reach for **it** rather than allow **it** the space to reach for **me**.

Our intent, the 3rd-century B.C.E. sage Antigonus Man-of-Sukot reminds us, should never be for the purpose of placating a one-eyed-purple-people-eater or to get a gold star of approval from God,[26] but to illuminate the darkness, to satisfy the longing of the emptiness, and to

---

[25] *Moral Grandeur and Spiritual Audacity*, p. 20

[26] *Mishnah, Avot* 1:3

calm the restlessness of the chaos. We should take on these endeavors because we are responsible stewards of this magnificent and most mysterious existence that has been abandoned at our doorstep and that is crying out to us, touching us at the deepest places of our hearts, pleading with us that we take it in, adopt it, choose it, welcome it, and guide it toward the realization of its optimal potentials.

Our wisdom is then in our willingness to be always aware that we are bereft of grasping the meaning of life and the purpose of our being, and to realize that even though we do not know *what* it is, we know *that* it is.[27]

"To be, or not to be," you see, is more than a question. It's a choice. And hopefully the wisdom scattered across these pages will help you with making it a good one.

---

[27] A.J. Heschel in *Moral Grandeur and Spiritual Audacity*, p. 11

Chapter Two

LOVE AND BARLEY

"There are no ugly trees; but there are
wormy fruits."[28]

A very long time ago, my people would do this ritual thing
every year during the two moons betwixt the beginning
of Spring and the beginning of Summer. They would take
the first yield of the earth in Spring, which happened to
be barley back then, and they would do stuff with it that
would make you dizzy, waving it back and forth and up
and down. And they would do this daily while counting
the days from the season of the first budding (Spring) to
the season of the full blossoming (Summer).[29]

What is the ritual of the barley offering?
One waves the barley shoots in its season,
first forward, then back, to ward off severe
winds; then toward the sky, and then
toward the earth to ward off severe rains.
In addition: First inward and outward
to the One to whom belongs all of the

---

[28] Abraham Joshua Heschel in *Man is not Alone*, p. 179
[29] Leviticus 23:11

universe, then upward and downward to the One who is Keeper of both the Upper Realms and the Lower Realms. Shimon bar Lakish remarked: "Let not the ritual of the barley offering be a light thing in your eyes, for it is through this ritual that God promotes harmony between a man and a woman."[30]

Fascinating. Lift up a handful of barley and wave it forward and backward, then up and down, and not only will you ward off severe winds and rains, but you will also improve your relationship with the opposite sex. Wow. What a ritual.

And of all things: **Barley**! You'd think, maybe a pomegranate, or a handful of chocolate-covered peanuts. But barley? What is this obsession with barley? Forty-nine days of barley is enough to ward off **any**thing, including an **appetite** for barley.

Here's another one: "If one dreams of barley, it is a sign that one's sins have been forgiven. Zey'ra (3rd century) longed so much to leave Babylon and relocate to Judea but refrained from doing so until he dreamed of barley."[31] And finally my favorite: "When the jar is empty of barley, conflict comes knocking at your door."[32]

So, my sense is that either these ancient teachers did something other than wave barley around, like maybe turn it into kegs of strong beer, or they were trying to teach

---

[30] *Midrash Pesikta D'Rav Kahana* 8:5 [*Pis'ka Chet, Ha'Omer*, para. 11]

[31] *Talmud Bavli, Berachot* 57a

[32] *Talmud Bavli, Baba Metzia* 59a

us something significant. And if the latter, perhaps it goes something like this:

As the first yield of Spring, barley represents First Love. When Jeremiah the Prophet interviewed God on an ancient rendition of "In-Treatment," he asked what it was that touched God the most about his first date. The reply: "I remember that the love we experienced was all-inclusive; my date threw all caution to the wind and followed me into the wilderness, into a place of no promise, no potential, no seed, no purpose, no plan, no definition. I remember it because it was unconditional, hinging on nothing but the purity of the moment. There was nothing between us but the innocence of trust and the passion of abandon." Jeremiah chiseled some notes on his serpentine clipboard and then inquired: "You mention all this 'innocent love' you felt. What do you mean by that?" God took in a deep breath and let out a Tsunami that wiped out four hotels in the Caribbean, and said: "The best way I can put it, is that it was like a Genesis, absent anything that ever was."[33]

Barley is like your first romance. Your first love. It represents the first move of earth in her romance with sky, responding to the rains of winter, reaching for the sky in total faith, in total innocence and trust, after which all else follows suit and emerges. Barley makes the first phone call, is the first to dare venture forth out of the earth of winter. And seeing that barley took a chance of emerging into the unknown, grass followed next, then wheat, then oats, then alfalfa, then little budding leaves peer hesitatingly from the tips of twigs, notice that it is

---

[33] Jeremiah 2:2-3

okay to take a chance and respond to the call of sky, to the impregnation of rain, to the love of Creator; to Craig's List.

And every single day, every single phase of that season of new beginnings, of fresh unfolding of Spring, was in ancient times celebrated with sheaves of barley, offerings of First Love. And we sent her message outward to the world, inward to our selves, up toward the heavens, down toward the earth, shooing away any harsh winds or rains that would try and come between us, that would try to stunt the magical emergence of fresh love, of renewed creation. And then we went home to our partners and didn't see them the same old way we had gotten used to seeing them. We saw them **anew** and remembered the love of our youth, the excitement we experienced during that first encounter at Applebee's.

And yes, of course your sins are forgotten when you dream of barley, because you have become so completely transformed; you have emerged from the constraints of Winter, and there is nowhere else to go now but toward full blooming and total blossoming. And if you have been hesitating to leave Cleveland for Milan, dreaming of barley would surely shake you out of your stupor and move you out of the hardened wood of twig into the soft, lush, color and fragrance of leaf.

But remember: Never **ever** let your barley run out. **Ever.** Else, you're liable to slip-slide back into old patterns, and your relationship will grow stale and the flame will flicker and the music will die and the apple will rot and the lights will go out and your remote will malfunction and you'll take your Chevy to the levee only to find the levee has dried.

The lesson around the ancient rite of "the Counting of the Days of the Barley Offering" is that the **struggles** we engage in the course of reaching for our dreams and hopes are worthy of acknowledgment no less than the actual, eventual **realization** of those dreams and hopes. For without the one there is not the other. Too often we focus exclusively on the objectives, reacting to the failure of its immediacy with frustration and impatience. One wonders if the apple seed, too, experiences this frustration and sense of dashed hopes as it grows first into a wooden stick that in no way resembles the apple which the TV infomercials promised it would become.

The **course** of our journey frequently does not so much as **hint** to the successful fruition of our **intent**. More often than not, the road to what we desire is riddled with every conceivable indication that what we want is **not** what we will get. (Like in some restaurants.) The period between the advent of Spring and that of Summer -- between the genesis of primal budding and the genesis of full blossoming -- is therefore a sacred period during which we can learn patience as well as faith in the **process**. And lest we forget this lesson in trust, the Hebrew ancestors would during this period of unfolding bring daily offerings of barley, a produce that was already actualized at the beginning of Spring, to remind the people that the end result of their endeavors is already available, albeit concealed within the mystery of a process yet in motion.

Ritually or not, we need to count each day and make each day count. For every single phase of our budding in life is precious, is an achievement all its own, whether we find ourselves in the phase of the seed, the root, the trunk, the branch, the twig, or the leaf. While the fully-ripe apple may be more celebrated than its earlier phase as leaf or twig or branch, the ritual of counting each day during the interval between spring and summer reminds us that every stage that **leads** from seed to apple deserves its own acknowledgment and celebration as well.

Think about it: How often do we whiz right by the stages and phases involved in achieving our goals, trampling on them and squashing them into insignificance, sometimes even disdain, our focus exclusively set upon the goal, the objective, the finish -- the **purpose**? This ancient wisdom reminds us to stop in the **middle** of the process, of the evolution, to recognize and acknowledge the miracle of the moment, because this very precious moment -- even though it appears at this time in disarray, like debris at a construction site -- is nonetheless an essential piece to the end-product that we so eagerly look forward to.

I recall so vividly how during a special well-attended banquet honoring the world-renowned spiritual master, Moshe Feinstein, we young disciples were hurriedly scampering from corridor to corridor in search of the elderly saint, for he was nowhere to be found, and all the esteemed guests and notable dignitaries were growing concerned. Finally, we found him. He was in the kitchen praising and blessing the otherwise ignored food preparers, floor sweepers, dish washers, and waiter staff – you know, all those forgotten links between the fancy invitation cards and the pompous event itself. Moshe Feinstein, however, did **not** forget them. For him, **all** of the pieces leading up to the climax held equal sanctity. For him, purpose was futile without meaning.

The fact is, that in the course of our lifetime we are never guaranteed we will live long enough to finish what we want to accomplish. No guarantee at all. We **are** guaranteed, however, that we will live long enough to **try**, to at the very least **begin** the process and become immersed in it. What we call "success" is not defined solely by the quality of **final** accomplishment; it is defined no less by the small, often frustrating phases that lead **toward** the accomplishment. God meets Moses not at Carnegie Hall wielding a dry martini but in the barren wilderness of Mid'yan wielding a flaming bush. The Ten Commandments (or fifteen according to Rabbi Mel Brooks) came down from the Heavens not in some lofty synagogue in Jerusalem, but in the blazing desert of Sinai, in no-man…uh…no-person's-land, on some obscure mountain, miles and miles **from** the Promised Land. God says to Moses: "Wherever you happen to be is holy enough" -- right here, right now, not any special shrine or auspicious moment, but right now and right where you are in your process[34] -- right smack dab where you are as you are reading these words – if you are *ready*.

Spring time, more than any other season is ripe for this learning, because in Spring we watch with great anxiety the gradual budding of leaves, the gradual unfolding of flowers, the gradual emergence from the earth of all that had vanished from sight in Winter. We thank God for every phase of every bud on every twig, for every phase of every tomato slowly making its way out of the earth toward one day meeting us face to face in all of its glory, embedded in a mouth-watering gluten-free, dairy-free

---

[34] Exodus 3:5

pizza. We take this time to uplift ourselves from feeling frustrated in our own processes, frustrated that we haven't **achieved** yet, reminding ourselves instead how it isn't **about** achievement, it is about **effort**, process, the phases along the way.[35] (This is great therapy for procrastinators.)

Back when I was a normative young yeshiva boy, one of my teachers, the late Efrayim Zeitchik (he was actually always on time), used to speak often about the **sanctity** of time, of seasons. He would remind us of the ancient teachings around conjuring, calling forth something that lies dormant, and that has been waiting in its state of potential to be called into realization at the right moment. Creation, he taught, never actually **happened**. Rather, it is continuously **happening**, and through myriad venues of myriad possibilities. At any given moment, for example, a single grass seed can be destined to grow dozens of feet tall or only a few inches, depending on the timing, on when it was that the wind blew and therefore where it was that the seed was blown -- to the plains of Kansas, or onto the front lawn of a suburban Houston home at the mercy of an overzealous lawn mower.

Every moment, he taught us, is a crossroad, a fork in the path of realization, a choice in how something or someone will become realized, and a choice in how a situation or person will unfold. Where you are in your life right now as you read this is a result of a choice you made at some point in your life which could just as easily have landed you somewhere else, reading something else, or as someone so different than who you have become that it would shock you if you could only *see* yourself.

---

[35] *Mishnah, Avot* 5:26

Every moment is more than a marker of time; it is an infinite galaxy of possibilities, each possibility having been created before time itself in the cauldron of Genesis, waiting forever for its turn to be called into existence and only at **that** very moment. No other moment will do. "Every moment," taught my teacher, "is a portal through which any given aspect of infinite Creation and possibility might emerge and manifest. In every single moment, therefore, your persona shifts; you are liberated from who you were until that moment -- free to transform, to become someone different. You look the same and feel no inherent difference, but know that you are **not** the same. Ever again."[36]

Like an old saying goes: "A person is judged in every single moment."[37] This is a great teaching for those who believe in a pending "Day of Judgment." If we are judged in every moment, then there won't be a scheduling overload by the time we get to the Heavenly Court, and no waiting. On another level, it means that our action in any given moment is not seen as a continuum, a link in a chain of earlier choices and actions but is "judged" for what it is in that very moment regardless of the moment or moments previous. Our capacity to become better, or worse, is a never-ending flux. To paraphrase a famous adage from the first-century, B.C.E. Hillel the Elder: "Don't be so sure of yourself until the day they carry your sorry ass to Fairlawn"[38] since at any moment the circumstances of your life can bring you to a portal through which you -- by

---

[36] *Toras HaNefesh*, p. 35
[37] *Talmud Bav'li, Rosh Hashanah* 16a
[38] *Mishnah, Avot* 2:4

your choice and action in that moment – conjure into manifestation a possibility that could transform you in that instant into someone diametrically opposed to how you've always known yourself.

Another ancient teaching puts it this way: "If a thief stole, and later decided to restore the stolen property to its owner, if the victim had long given up on ever retrieving what was stolen, the theft remains a theft, and the return of the item is considered as if it was simply a gift."[39] In other words, had the thief returned the stolen items earlier, when the hope of restoration was still alive in the mind of the victim alongside the victim's pain of having been violated; had the thief acted in the moment that the thief felt the wrongness of their action, closer to the time of the act itself -- then the return of the theft would be just that and it would suffice as restitution and penance. In that moment, the portal of opportunity for transformation, for conjuring yet one more spark of the light of Genesis, remained open. But by the time the victim had given up all hope, however noble the intent of the reformed thief in returning the stolen property months later, it is too late to see it in that light. It becomes then a mere gift, the arbitrary act of some stranger showing up out of the blue and presenting a **gift**, not the ennobling act of a remorseful thief returning a stolen item; not the powerful act of reversing a wrong.

This may be a very difficult and challenging idea for some of us to absorb. (So take it with food.) It defies linear thinking. It baffles the mind. It shakes our ordinary way of thinking. It gives us a headache. Yet, Rav Zeitchik would

---

[39] *Talmud Bav'li, Baba Metzia* 26a

stress, "no moment in time has the power to rectify, alter, or in any way interfere with any other moment in time, having its **own** portals of opportunity to deal with, its own seeds of possibility that wait to be conjured."[40] Or as the ancient masters put it: "If you commit a wrong and then perform a good deed, the good deed does not cancel out the wrong."[41] It's not math; it's life. Once the moment has passed, it's gone. **Poof!** Not even the *Geek* Squad can recover it. So, don't waste your time and energy trying to retrieve it while neglecting the gifts of fresh opportunity that await in the **next** moments.

Deep food for thought. Both exhilarating, empowering, agitating, debilitating, intimidating – every moment a Genesis, an opportunity for a whole fresh start -- I can never un-do what I've done. Nonetheless, while I cannot un-do what I've done, I can commit to not repeating it, and can become a whole new person **incapable** of repeating it. And in so doing, I transform all the wrongs of my past, since I would never have arrived at the crossroads of my transformation had it not been for how I chose to deal with my mistakes **now**. This, and other factors, such as the weather, led the 2nd-century Shim'on bar Lakish to teach that when we change our ways in earnest and become better, we in that moment transform as well all of our wrongs of the past, for it is upon their backs that we have then reconstructed ourselves.[42] (We may of course be powerless to un-do what we did, reverse the pain we

---

[40] *To'rat HaNefesh*, p. 40
[41] *Midrash Yal'kot Mishlei*, No. 547
[42] *Talmud Bav'li, Yo'ma* 86b

caused others, but we can always sue them for the distress they've caused us by making us feel guilty.)

Now we understand more the intent behind the cryptic reading in the Bible: "These are the seasons of [God] that you should be calling forth in their appointed times..." What does that mean -- "Calling forth"? Do any of us have the power to "call forth" seasons? Or anything else? Rather, it means that for everything there is a season, an appointed time for it to be conjured into manifestation, even when it isn't politically-correct.

Even a **wrong** committed at the right time, the ancients taught -- at the right moment when the portal of Genesis is open for it to become manifest -- is considered "a beautiful happening in its appointed time."[43] I know. That's taking it too far. But take a moment and think about it. Let's say a man robs his wife of her life savings and invests it in a slot machine in Vegas and wins. So, although his actions are wrong, the moment is right, and he will return home with a wad full of *Ben Franklins*! How beautiful **indeed**! The beauty of it is that **she** will have more money than she ever dreamed of, and **he** will be able to afford the alimony. So, all is well.

Okay. Maybe that was not the best analogy. Maybe what these ancient sages meant to say was that even if your choice is wrong, you can refurbish the moment. You can in the moment of your *boo-boo* turn things around by redirecting the wrongness of your action toward rightness. So, you come home and find the skateboard in the walkway to your house and you lose it and yell at the kids: "*Who put the Goddam skateboard in the walkway*?!*" Instantly, in

---

[43] *Midrash Kohelet Rabbah* 3:15

the **moment**, you realize the wrongness of hurting your children's feelings over so trivial a phenomenon as having almost broken your leg, fractured your hip, herniated your discs and dislocated your shoulder, and so you quickly **transform** the moment by adding: "That is the cleverest thing I have ever seen! What a great idea!!! This way, I can get to the front **door** faster! **Thank** you!"

See? At first, you did a bad thing, but the moment opened up for you right then to create a whole new scenario, to call forth the primordial Light of Genesis from out of the primordial Darkness of Nemesis. Nothing more beautiful than that.

Every moment is then **eternal** in the sense that in that very moment we can begin anew, alter our fate, our destiny, with one swoop of a choice, of an in-the-moment decision. Interestingly, the word for "moment" in the ancient Hebrew language is exactly the same as the word for "invitation" – z'mahn. Every moment is an invitation waiting for your RSVP.

Therefore, even though much of my life is out of my control, I can still focus on any given **moment** and make that moment special, sacred, larger-than-life, severing the experience of it from the ongoing saga of my life-problems. I can accept the invitation and attend, open to both its gifts and its challenges, remembering that flowers grow from dirt, and diamonds must be cut, and I've got to crack the shell to eat the nut, and that my plate of healthy veggies were made possible by a pile of manure.

Legend has it that when Caesar Publius Aelius Hadrianus was en-route through Judea to do battle against some dissenters 1900 years ago, he noticed an elderly gentleman busily planting a fig tree. He halted his horse and asked the elder his age. "I am 100 years old," the man replied. "Well, then why do you bother planting?" asked Hadrianus. After all, the Roman leader laughed, the old man would never live long enough to see his sapling grow and bear fruit! So why bother? The elder replied that if he doesn't live another couple of years to see it bear fruit, at least his children and grandchildren would.[44]

This story is about focusing in on the gift of the moment without being distracted by the down-side of our assumptions of the future, or the "result." We see this in an earlier teaching, in the ancient writ of the Hebrew prophet Jeremiah, where in his prophecy around the looming exile of his people to Babylon, he quotes God as saying: "I just exiled you from Jerusalem to Babylon. So, sue me. But what I suggest is that you busy yourselves with building homes there, and settling in them, and planting gardens, and continue perpetuating families, children, etc. and seek the peace of the place to which I have exiled you...."[45]

In other words, even though the future looked bleak -- exile, the destruction of their independent commonwealth, subjection to another culture, etc. – the Hebrews were implored to not allow the bleak forecast to dampen the gift of the moment, and were instead encouraged to make the **best** of the situation, build homes in the exile, start families, plant gardens, orchards, and not get caught up in what **might** be or in what might have **been**, but in what **is**; to seek out the gift of the moment and then seize it. This is one of the mysteries behind why the Jewish people are still

---

[44] *Midrash Tanchuma, Kedoshim*, Ch. 8

[45] Jeremiah 29:4-7

around while all the high-and-mighty empires that hoped for their destruction are currently sealed behind glass in your local museum, and why religions who thought they'd replaced the Jews and their ancient Covenant have – to this day – been continuously clamoring to contrive new and improved rationales around why the Jews and their supposedly defunct Judaism still exist. Like the Phoenix, they kept rising from out of the ashes because of this wisdom about meaning *sans* purpose and about the sanctity of Moment. This is in fact the wisdom of the Phoenix.

Speaking of the Phoenix, let me share an ancient story about it.

A long long time ago, long before time was ago, there was a great flood that swept across our earth and swallowed everything and everyone in one huge catastrophic gulp. Nothing survived, no one was left alive, except this one family and all the species of animals and plants they had managed to gather onto their crudely-built boat.

Floating on the surface of the waters, the family was busy day and night feeding the animals with what they'd gathered before the flood, comforting the traumatized and treating the sick.

The family's elder was a man known as Noah, ancient Hebrew for "console" or "ease." He shuffled through the boat at all hours making sure every creature was okay.

Over many days and many rounds, Noah shuffled past a mythic creature known as the Phoenix, a bird-like creature that eluded definition and always remained quietly crouched in the corner of the boat, never uttering a word, never moving. Noah never noticed the Phoenix until one day when he took a moment and stopped to take a breath. And he noticed.

"You have never asked for anything," he said to the Phoenix. "Why is that? I don't ever remember even feeding you all these weeks!"

The Phoenix looked up at the weary old man and replied: "I am aware of the awesome magnitude of your responsibility here. I watch you daily, notice how hard you work at taking care of everyone. I did not want to add to your burden."

When Noah heard these words, he crouched to look the Phoenix in the eyes and said: "Thank you for noticing. For by so doing, you have brought me back to my heart of hearts. You have restored me to awareness of my being, an awareness I have lost over the many days and hours during which I have busily tended to everyone. Everyone but myself. You have reminded me of who I am; you have resurrected my soul."

With tears in his eyes, Noah then placed his leathery hands on the head of the Phoenix and blessed the Phoenix: "In return, may you never lose your own essence, the gift of your selfhood, not in the whirlwind of time nor in the tumultuousness of day-to-day survival. In dying may you rediscover life anew; in falling may you rise to ever-renewing heights."

As soon as he'd finished blessing the Phoenix, Noah noticed. He noticed everything -- his body, his breathing, his family, all the animals, the plants. Most amazingly, he noticed it had stopped raining, and that the floodwaters were receding. And that the earth had not been destroyed after all.

"What a gift in itself," he whispered, "to notice. To simply notice. Thank you, Phoenix. Thank you."

"Your gratitude," the Phoenix corrected him, "belongs only to yourself, old man. For the gift of noticing began with you; when you finally took a moment. It was then that you noticed **me**."[46]

Looking out the window of the boat Noah noticed the rain clouds dissipating, and as they did so they formed the shape of the Phoenix and then receded, enabling the sunshine to reach the earth. When he looked back down at where the Phoenix was crouched, it was gone. And then he knew. The Phoenix was the spirit of the earth. And this realization comforted him greatly, for as the Phoenix would never die, neither would the earth; she would only rise again and again to ever-renewing Life. If only we would never cease to notice her, to acknowledge her. That's all it would take. And to do so with ourselves and with each other. To take a moment now and then. And never let it go.

This is what it means to live a meaningful life without purpose.

---

[46] The original tale appears in *Talmud Bav'li, Sanhedrin* 108a

Chapter Three

WHY CAMELS DON'T HAVE HORNS

> "Our life is beset by difficulties, yet it
> is never devoid of meaning."[47]

Listen carefully. You are an original. You are like no other. Never in the history of humanity was there ever anyone exactly like you, nor will there **ever** be. You are the exclusive version of you. A "Limited Edition." You're like a snowflake. No two snowflakes are alike, no two fingerprints, no two DNA structures.

"If I am so unique," you then ask, "so **special**, then what is my **purpose**?"

Listen. Purpose is overrated. What is it your business what purpose God, or Intelligent Design, or Darwin had in mind when the idea of **you** came up? What makes you think that your right to life hangs on some kind of particular task, and that you were specifically hired to perform it? And anyway, if you knew why you were here, what would be the point in you **being** here, altogether?

---

[47] A.J. Heschel in *Moral Grandeur and Spiritual Audacity*, p. 11

Basically, you are here for the purpose of not knowing why. So deal with it.

My ancestors have this tradition about one of our tribal chieftains you may know of as "King David" -- who lived back some 3,000 years ago. One day, while meditating out in the Judean Desert, he turned to the heavens and declared: "Master of the Universe! Please reveal to me the way in which you wish me to live." Replied God: "Just *do* and *eat*!"[48]

You want purpose? There's your purpose. Do and eat. Case closed.

Really? It's not all about worship and spirituality? It's not about seeking purpose and significance? It's not about achieving and succeeding? Not at all, taught the ancient masters. The most fundamental principle of life is: "Do and eat." Or, in the words of another like adage: "The Compassionate One says, 'Just *do*! And whatever it is you find to do, it will be pleasing to me.'"[49]

Clearly, the wise ones intended by these teachings to yank the rug of presumptions from under us so that we might hear in the silence and feel in the absence the very unique resonance of our very own individual and distinctive Self that might have gotten drowned out in the collective noise of life's otherwise boisterous pomp and circumstance.

"You want to know my desire for how you ought to live?" God asks. "It's quite simple. *Do* something with the life I gave you. **Any**thing. *You* create it this time, from your essential self, your very own intuition. I'll send the

---

[48] *Midrash Tehilim*, Chapter 16, para. 6
[49] *Talmud Bav'li*, *B'choro't* 17b

wind, but **you** set the sail. Lend your ear to your own heart for a change rather than surrender it to external voices and to the expectations of others. And **eat**; enjoy this beautiful world I gifted to you, and the delicious senses of your body and the means of relishing your senses with which I have endowed you. I have no need for your worship of *me*,[50] your attention to *me*, and I deplore your obsession with second-guessing what *I* want. I am actually more pleased by what you yourself come up with that brings quality and meaning and joy to *you!* So, **surprise** me!"

The fourth-century master, Rav Zechariah, once declared: "In the future, we will have to account before Creator for all the pleasures of life we wanted to partake of [legal, of course], had the opportunity to partake of, but **didn't**."[51]

Our purpose, **all** of us, is to **be**. How we go about doing that is a very personal choice born out of each our uniqueness. The big challenge is dealing with all of the distractions that come our way, luring us to become other than who and what we are, in exchange for which we often end up bartering essential qualities of our selfhood and in the process of which we consequently whittle away at our originality, our distinctiveness, the very special and exclusive version of us that was forged in the Cauldron of Genesis from the beginning of time.

One of the many animal fables I remember growing up with is the one about Camel. Camel, you see, felt slighted by Creator for not having been issued horns like most other cud-chewing animals. He also had a negative image

---

[50] Psalms 50:9-12

[51] *Talmud Yerushalmi, Kidushin*, end of Ch. 4

of himself because of his humped back. And so he set out on a long journey to find a pair of horns for himself. Eventually, he met Gazelle, and noticed how beautiful Gazelle's horns were, how regal he appeared with those graceful, curvy horns. Camel decided right then and there he was going for the "Gazelle look."

Camel wasted no time in asking Gazelle what it would take to sport a pair of horns like his. Gazelle examined Camel and said: "You'll have to lose your ears to make room for our kind of horns." Camel grew worried. "If you remove my ears, how will I be able to listen-out for the possible approach of predators? Isn't there any other option?"

Gazelle paraded around Camel a few times, examining every inch of him, and finally said: "The eyelids, then. Your eyelids take up too much space on your head. If we can reduce the size of...."

"My **eye**lids?!" Camel interrupted. "Don't you realize how badly I need those eyelids for the sand storms?!"

Gazelle thought for a moment and exclaimed: "Your hump! If we remove the hump off your back, we can probably fashion out of it a set of horns far taller and more majestic than even **mine**!"

Again, Camel protested: "My **hump**? I **need** my hump. It is the only way I can survive for *days* in the desert until I find the next water-hole!"

"How about those sharp little tusks you have in your mouth? We can remove those, plant them on your head, and with time they will grow into beautiful horns like mine!"

"No," Camel protested. "I need those sharp teeth to

pry thorns and hard-to-pluck vegetation in the desert, or I would starve!"

Gazelle gave Camel a friendly poke with his horns and said: "Don't you see how well-equipped you are? How blessed you are with so many means of thriving and surviving within the framework of your particular life circumstances?? You ought to be **proud** of yourself! You have everything you need, including a pair of sharp tusk-like teeth with which you can bite anyone trying to attack you, let alone avail yourself of varieties of desert plant food. You don't need horns. You need to feel privileged to have been gifted with all that you already **have!**"

Camel nodded. Gazelle was right. He had everything he needed and then some. Thanking Gazelle, Camel walked off toward his home in the distant desert.

And that is why, to this day, camels walk with their heads held high in pride, and with that smug smile on their faces. They are proud of all the many faculties with which they are endowed like no other creature on Earth.

So, purpose *schmurpose*. We need to revel as much in the fact that we **don't** have horns as Gazelle revels in the fact that he **does**.

Chapter Four

THE SCAPEGOAT AND
THE ILLUSIONIST

I know. I am aware that some of you are still stuck with the earlier story of Adam and Eve, waiting for me to so much as mention the notorious *Serpent* who talked them into eating of the Forbidden Fruit to begin with. Please know that I have not forgotten him. He is very important to our life journey and the meaning we bring to it – or don't.

But first: Have you ever had one of those days or nights during which you find yourself worrying for hours on end about a matter you're not even sure is actually cause for worrying? Say, the gas pump doesn't fill your tank all the way one day, and you interpret this to mean your credit card's been maxed which is impossible because you know you've got cash in the bank to cover it, so it could only mean that your account may have been hacked and you're now in the hole and have to call the bank in the morning to deal with all of this and get a whole new card and examine your bank statement to contest fraudulent charges, and you go to bed worrying, turning and twisting all night wondering how did this happen, and why, and what are you going to use to fill up your near-empty tank and get to work tomorrow and how are you going to buy groceries and pay the rent which is due in two days, not to mention the phone bill which is dangerously overdue and threatening to cut you off from all communication with the rest of Planet Earth?

And then, and then the next day you find out that actually your money's still in your account, **with** interest, and that it was probably just a faulty gas pump, and all is well, and you lost sleep – not to mention years off your designated life span -- worrying over absolutely nothing.

I firmly believe that this is what happened to the Biblical character *Eee'yo'v* (a/k/a "Job"). The Book of Job is about some guy who had everything and then lost it all because of a wager God made with one of his top angels. Most of you know this angel as a **bad** sort of guy, namely "Satan," or "The Devil", or "Lucifer." Truth be told, he's had a bad rap, thanks to the zeal of religious hype and sorely misguided theologies. In my people's language he is known as *ha'satan*, literally: "The Obstructer." He is an angel like any other, with a mission assigned him by God Itself. His mission is to call your bluff and test your conviction. So be nice and stop blaming all your ills on him.

I am going to say this only once: *He **didn't** make you do it.*

Ha'satan's wager with God was that he could get Job so pissed-off that Job would break down and reveal his true character from beneath all his purported "saintliness" and *curse* God. God then accepts the bet and authorizes *ha'satan* to go do his thing, which he does by stripping Job of all of his assets, at home and abroad – including his hidden Hedge Funds – then striking him with some god-awful disease which caused him to lose his health insurance, and depriving him of everything and everyone he'd ever cherished. In the end, *ha'satan* **loses** the bet, but only after tormenting us with 36 chapters in which Job and his friends philosophize around the question of why he had to endure all of this needless suffering in the **first** place, or why bad things happen to good people.

Now, what if Job never actually lost **any**thing? What if none of what the story describes actually occurred, and Job got sick from worrying as intensely as he did over what he *believed* had happened, but which in reality **didn't**? After all, nowhere in the entire story is there a clear indication that any of the stuff Job was **told** happened, actually **happened**. All we are told is that some anonymous character or another showed up day after day with increasingly horrifying news alleging that such-and-such occurred. But never is there any mention of the occurrence *itself* outside of the hearsay delivered by a successive host of unnamed messengers.

Could it be that the unnamed characters who kept showing up in various guises with ever-intensifying news were none other than *ha'satan* and his cadre busily trying to **trip** Job? Does Job set off to investigate these reports? Does he attend so much as a single funeral? Not at all. He falls apart at the reports, accepts them as truths and descends deeper and deeper into a sink-hole of utter despair hollowed-out by the "reports." His suffering, his grieving, is so real that his friends come over to sit with him and comfort him, for they too have been swept up in the whirlwind that now has their hapless friend spinning out of control. And so, for 36 long and dense chapters we are forced to listen to Job and his well-meaning friends pontificate and theorize why it is that Job has been strapped with a series of ghastly tragedies that may not have occurred **after** all!

In the end, I envision The Satan throwing up his arms in utter frustration, bored out of his angelic skull by all the philosophizing going on in Job's living room day after day but still feeling somewhat successful in that he at least got Job to *think* he'd lost everything even though he hadn't lost **any**thing.

In the end, as the story has it, God appears to Job "from out of the whirlwind," from out of the spin that Job is in, from out of the storm of assumption and of all the havoc it had wrought. In the end, God does not **heal** Job, because Job isn't really sick. It's all in his head. Job becomes "healed" by God wrenching him out of his spin, out of the illusion he had created for himself by way of his worry-ridden assumptions. Also in the end, God does not answer Job's questions of "Why?" Because to respond to questions would be tantamount to acknowledging that there are any. And in truth, all of our questions – again -- are predicated upon assumptions we ourselves have invented.

In the end, everything and everyone Job thought he lost are restored to him manifold more than they were before, meaning he came away with a deeper appreciation for his daughters, his sons, his herds, his fields, his employees, and so on. Not that God waved a wand and suddenly daughters and sons appeared from out of nowhere. On the contrary, they appeared from where they'd been meandering all along. While Job had been mourning them, they had been happily prancing about in Reno or the Caribbean, and his allegedly-abducted field workers had been joyfully gyrating at a Grateful Dead Concert in the Land of Oz. And no animals were hurt in the making of this story.

And if you are wondering in your skeptical mind how it is possible for such a holy and enlightened and spiritually evolved master like Job to have fallen for *ha'satan's* illusionistic tricks, and to such a **degree**! --then remember how the Torah describes *ha'satan* in the guise of the Edenic Serpent as "the most cunning of all creations,"[52] so incredibly cunning, in fact, that he was able to successfully talk the first human couple into partaking of the very fruit of which they were specifically instructed by Creator just twenty minutes earlier *not* to partake. If Adam and Eve, the direct handiwork of God, could fall for the web of illusion spun by *ha'satan*, so much more so is it feasible that Job could and would as well.

Ha'satan – or The Satan -- is an illusionist par-excellence. The best there is and ever was. It's his job; his role in the scheme of things; the very purpose for which he was created: to challenge always our snug take on reality, our convictions, our self-proclaimed truths and home-brewn presumptions. If he can dupe Adam and Eve, he can dupe Job.

Mystics like the 18th-century Nachmon of Breslav, referred to The Satan as *ko'ach ha'me'dameh*, "The Force of Similitude," the force that can render what **is** as *not* and what is **not** as *is*. The Satan is the illusionist-*par-excellence*,

---

[52] Genesis 3:1

capable of making nothing *appear* as if it were something, and something *appear* as if it were nothing. In the original Hebraic narrative of the Adam and Eve story, it took Snake only *seventeen* words to undo what God had decreed in *eighteen* words. It is amazing. Because illusion, you see, is but only a single tiny step *short* of reality. It is close enough a degree of *Almost* to practically resemble with uncanny precision that which in reality it is not.

Verily I say unto you, nothing actually happened to Job. Snake was just doing his thing and pulling the wool over Job's eyes. The narrative does not describe anything actually **happening** to anyone, only that one messenger after another shows up on Job's front porch with reports of one fiasco after the other.[53] The first of these "messengers" is described in the Hebrew as *mal'ach* which translates both as "Messenger" and as "Angel" – take your pick. In other words, an angel – The Satan? – came to him with the report, and then another angel – of The Satan's crew? -- or The Satan in a variety of disguises? -- and then another and another. No mention of Job dialing 9-1-1 and then dashing off to investigate, or to bury his supposedly dead children, or to gather neighbors and kinsmen to try and retrieve the stolen herds or abducted shepherds. He just falls apart on the spot and blesses God instead of cursing.

Failing to trip Job and get him to *curse* God, Snake gets more physical and makes him think he's sick, and it's so real for him that he breaks out in boils, but he still goes to shul and board meetings. This guy is hard to crack. You can **fool** him but you can't break him.

In the end, as in the beginning, Job has three

---

[53] Job 1:14-18

daughters and seven sons.[54] Nothing's changed. Nothing's changed because nothing happened. Nor does it say that God increased for Job double of what he *lost*. Rather, it says "And God increased everything that was [already] unto Job, double their number." But he still had the same number of daughters and sons, except now Job's eyes are open, his heart has been renewed, he sees life differently, he has been redeemed from out of the whirlwind, a whirlwind which The Satan had fanned into a Tsunami but which Job himself had seeded in presuming too much about what God wants. So much so, in fact, that he would regularly offer up sin-offerings on behalf of his party-loving children just in case they got too naughty during one of their wild bashes.[55]

Not anymore, though. Following his debacle, Job has now been exposed to the God who is anything *but* exacting, the God who leaves us ample room for error, and who would rather that Job focus more on the needs of his family not in terms of what he assumes they owe God, but in terms of what it is they owe themselves for bettering the quality of their lives. Job becomes more sensitive to the honor and dignity of his daughters, for instance, than constantly worrying about the honor of God. God cannot be slighted, Job learns; but people can. Having now learned this after his lengthy and intensive stroll with God who cherishes her Creations in Chapters 38 and on, Job's daughters are now *named*, and described as "the most beautiful in all the land," and apportioned their own 20-acre homesteads whereas in the beginning

---

[54] Job 1:2 and 42:13
[55] Job 1:5

they were nameless squatters at the homes of their equally nameless and anonymous brothers.[56]

The wool over our eyes, you see, can either leave us forever blinded and weighed down or gift us with renewed vision and fortitude. It is up to us, to how we respond once we realize we've been duped. We can in that moment fall, or rise. "And the eyes of them both [Adam and Eve] were awakened, and they became aware that they were naked."[57] Adam and Eve did indeed push through the wool that was pulled over their eyes by Snake, and they did indeed come out the other side, like Job would, and with fresh, renewed perspective. ("Original Sin" is in neither the vocabulary nor the theology of the tradition in which that story originated.)

The Illusionist, you see, thrives on our attachment to the world of imagery and appearances, on our draw to or repulsion from what things "look like." He takes advantage of our obsession with expression, with mastering the art of communication, our self-confidence or the lack thereof. He is after all the first of God's creations to initiate, to take a first step, to open communications. He invented **Question**. He kindled **Response**. He developed **Dialogue**. He was the most "naked" of all creatures, reads the original Hebrew narrative in its literal translation.[58] Cunning *schmunning*. He was more *naked* than anything God ever created, meaning he was so totally emotionally and intellectually honest and open that you'd have wanted to marry him straightaway *regardless* of your sexual orientation. He is

---

[56] Job 1:4

[57] Genesis 3:7

[58] Genesis 3:1

The Illusionist, the *ko'ach ha'me'dah'meh*, the Power of Similitude.

And you can't live with him or without him. Not in **this** world. Not in the Garden of Paradox. He is your ticket to Heaven or to Hell -- which are in essence one and the same -- for he is willing to negotiate your trip to either for the same price. He is your guide to the Tree of Life or the Tree of Knowledge – which are in essence one and the same tree -- for he is naked, more naked than you can possibly imagine, and he enjoys helping you see what you want to see. And to keep himself as naked as possible he sheds his skin periodically, and like a master initiating a disciple, he drops his shed skin for you to find and to don, for you to wear over your own nakedness lest you become overwhelmed by it. This way, you can walk about making-believe you're as naked as he, while all along veiling all that you prefer not to expose of your deepest Shadow Self.

He is the spiritual embodiment of all that is homeopathic. He is poison; he is medicine. He calls your bluff. He puts your conviction to the test. He is The *Satan*, an extremely high and important Angel of God who has been demonized by religion and tabooed by most of humankind through most of human history. He is Sama'el, *sama* meaning "blinding," and also "potion." Potions can heal; potions can kill. Darkness is blinding, and so is too much Light. He is the juggler of both ends of the same stick, Keeper of Polarities, Dancer of the Spectrums, Master of Illusions. He is neither good nor evil. He is both.

And in very ancient times, on *Yom Kippur* –the holiest of the holiest of days for my people -- we used to invite him to our Ceremony of Atonement and accord him an equal share of the main dish we served to Creator: Goat. We sent one goat to God, and one to The Illusionist, both goats symbolic of all of The Illusionist's successes in causing us to stumble and trip all over ourselves, causing us to feel that what we did wrong was okay – in the moment – and then leaving us hanging with the pain of regret and the anguish of remorse the morning after. And for this, we rewarded him with what has over time come to be known as a "scapegoat," a sort of bribe to "destroy the original negatives." Literally.

The ritual of selecting which goat was to be offered to God and which to The Illusionist played-out like a public magic show, a performance in which the High Priest appeared to take the place of The Illusionist. He stood in front of a small box in which lots were placed, two pieces of boxwood inscribed either with the words "For YHWH" or the words "For Aza'zel."[59] Two goats were then positioned on either side of him, one to his left and one to his right. He would then reach into the box and mix up the pieces so that he no longer knew which one was for the goat on the right, which for the goat on the left. Then he blindly reached both hands into the box and quickly, spontaneously, and without thinking about it or in any way hesitating, withdrew both pieces of boxwood simultaneously, one in each hand. If, for instance, his left hand held the piece marked "For YHWH," the goat on his left would be designated for the altar, and the goat on the right for Aza'zel, and vice-versa.[60]

---

[59] Leviticus 16:8-10 and 21-23

[60] *Talmud Bav'li, Yoma* 37a and *Mishnah, Yoma* 3:10

After sending the spirit of the one goat to God, the High Priest would then lay his hands upon the **second** goat, the "scapegoat" – actually referred to in the Hebrew as *se'ir ha'chai* -- "*Living* Goat" – and assign it into the care of a designated *eesh ee'tee*, literally: "A Man of Season," meaning someone who is ready, prepared, really present in the moment to engage whatever, whenever, however. The ancient mystics described this character as having bushy eyebrows, blue eyes that are crooked and asymmetrical, with one eye being smaller than the other.[61] These facial features would indicate to the High Priest that he was the right man for the job (and don't ask me why). The bushy eye-browed, blue-eyed, crooked-eyed, asymmetrical-eyed designee would then lead the Living Goat across the Judean hills way into the nakedness place, to an undesignated designated site in the desert, where he would release the goat to the **Master** of Nakedness, The Illusionist, referred to by the Torah narrative as "Aza'zel." And *wa la*! **Poof**! Sins are gone. Vanished!

In this annual drama of the Day of Atonement, God represents the actual dissipation of our sins while Aza'zel represents the earthly fact that even though our sins are no more, there remain ample memories of them strewn all about the labyrinth of our ongoing life journey – in the backroads of the memories of our minds, as the song goes -- for, again, we live in the realm of attachments, and it's hard to let go, to truly **truly** let go. The "Living Goat" who symbolically carries our mistakes into the desert, into the void, takes them as far away as possible, out of sight, but is still a "living" goat nonetheless. Our past is

---

[61] Zohar, Vol. 3, folio 63b

gone, vanished, but what carries it is still alive, trekking through the wilderness toward Aza'zel in the hope that The Illusionist will, again, "burn the negatives" and free us of what he otherwise lords over our heads—or of what we call "guilt."

Whether all of this is to be taken literally or not is moot against the awesome backdrop of the wisdom gleaned from this primitive shamanic ceremony. The ancient teachers read into it any number of concepts and interpretations because that's our way. We don't just make bread out of the raw gift of wheat or barley. We also make cupcakes and cereal and beer. Likewise, the sages drew from a rainbow of perspectives, some seeing the Aza'zel ceremony as a gesture of atonement for the Fallen Angels of Genesis 6:4 who symbolize the overwhelming force of the sensuous. The sensuous, they felt, often burns so fiercely within us that we are led to make wrong choices out of the sway of our natural terrestrial impulses, impulses so potent they even lured Heavenly Angels out of their hoity-toity celestial Paradise.[62] Others saw the ritual as the necessary act of inviting the forces of evil into the ceremony of the sacred as a gesture of unifying all of the polarities of our mysterious universe.[63] And yet others, like the 18th-century Shimshon Rafael Hirsch, interpreted the observance as very directly addressing the day-to-day downhome nitty-gritty in-the-moment struggle of right or wrong choice-making:

---

[62] *Talmud Bav'li, Yoma* 67b; Book of Enoch 10:4,5

[63] Zohar, Vol. 3, folio 63a

Clearly, we have here a description of two creatures which at the outset are identical in every respect but which come to a complete parting of the ways once they arrive at the threshold of the Sanctuary. They are both identical in appearance, size and monetary value. Both were purchased at the same time. Both are placed in the same manner "before God in the entrance of the Tent of Appointed Meeting." The lot marked "for God" or that "for Aza'zel" could fall upon either one of them. The chances of becoming the one or the other are the same for each. Indeed, each of the two can only become that which it will become because it could just as well have become the other.....Thus, all of us are placed into the entrance of His Sanctuary, without distinction [to decide] between YHWH and Aza'zel, between God and the powers of our senses....This choice is not made for any of us in advance. Physical appearances, physical stature, financial status, higher or lower social standing, greater or lesser affluence, even the circumstances under which we are called upon to make our choices – none of these have a compelling influence on our decision. Respected or obscure, great or humble, rich or poor, today or tomorrow, no matter what his powers or possessions – anyone can become either "onto YHWH" or "onto Aza'zel" at any time…. Indeed, the very enticements of Aza'zel should have led him to God, for without these temptations he could never have become the free-willed [son or daughter] and servant of God, of the free-willed Holy One.[64]

However you slice it, it boils down to this: We are all cast into a narrow box in which we meander about between two pieces of boxwood, one marked for God, one for Aza'zel. This is what it looks like inside of us. On the outside, we stand tall and majestic, like the High Priest of antiquity, ready to chance our next move with an air of awe and audacity. Two equally attractive or equally foreboding choices are brought to us and positioned on either side of us as we take a deep breath and quickly reach into our deepest innards with both possibilities in mind and do our best with whatever and however the consequences of our action might turn out. In most every choice we make, we have to end up sending a part of our Self out to the unknown perils of the wilderness abode of Aza'zel, even if we first sent another part of our Self to the highest and most noble reaches of intents – that is, even if we made the most correct and most gallant of choices.

In every choice, then, there is sacrifice, for better or for worse, or for both. This, I believe, underlies all of the rituals of the sacrificial rites of my ancestors. They were meant to teach us this important life lesson. The altars,

---

[64] *The Pentateuch* [Abridged One-Volume Version], pp. 436-438

the animals, the blood, the dead-bird/live-bird rituals, the live-goat/dead-goat rituals, the red-cow-ashes rituals, the sacred fire and incense rituals -- all of them were intended not for the altars of earth and stone but for the far more sacred altars of heart and soul. Their meaning remains precious and have empowered us to survive thousands of years of disillusionment, because they remain always the antidote to the cunningness of The Illusionist; they remain always the trick in tricking the Trickster.

Job, you see, was a passionate, devoted ritual-sacrificer. He had one sacrifice or another smoldering on his altar almost every other day, bribing God to forgive his party-loving kids just in case they erred. Just in case. He had no idea whether they actually did or not. He was tangled-up in the power of illusion and assumption. All of his subsequent questions regarding what God did or didn't do, or should or shouldn't have done, were all predicated on his illusory presumptions about God, Life, and Job. He was so totally a victim of The Illusionist that all it took The Satan to get him grieving and sick was hearsay, some anonymous Blog, something he'd read on Google or seen on YouTube.

Yom Kippur is more than an ancient biblical Israelite ceremony. It is a universal lesson that reminds us to transform our Scapegoat Selves into *Living* Goats, and The Illusionist into our Teacher. *With* him alone we **are** nothing, for he overshadows our Selfhood. With*out* him altogether we *learn* nothing, for he also *empowers* our Selfhood. It all depends on whether we stand up there like a half-assed *Almost*-High-Priest with only *one* piece of boxwood in the container before us and one solitary goat by our side, or whether we stand boldly as the fully-empowered and anointed High Priest before the concealed encasement of Choice with two unequalled pieces of boxwood and two **equal** goats at either side, ready to walk the tightrope between the Angel of Light and the Angel of Darkness, remembering always that both work for the same boss and that both have your best interest in mind and that both are actually one and the same and that their seeming difference is nothing more than an…illusion. No less than the man with the big eye and the small eye is still one and the same guy, his asymmetrical eyes, bushy eyebrows and crooked glance notwithstanding.

To get this difficult concept across with a tad more clarity I'm going to tell you the story of Plimo.[65]

Plimo was a righteous man who lived in Jerusalem in the first century, B.C.E. He was a wealthy and very successful merchant known for his charitable ways, and he was blessed with a beautiful family and a huge, luxurious abode. As part of his daily religious devotion, he would ask God to please keep The Satan away from him and from his family, and then he would proclaim: "An arrow in your eye, O Dark Angel!" And thus he went about satisfied that he'd driven away any impulse toward sinfulness by his daily bold appellations against The Illusionist.

One Yom Kippur Eve, when Plimo sat comfortably around his dinner table surrounded by his honorable guests and his perfect family, a filthy disheveled vagabond arrived, knocking ferociously on Plimo's 2,100-year-old door. As you know, on the eve of this holiest day of the year we are encouraged to celebrate with a lavish feast

---

[65] *Talmud Bav'li, Kidushin* 81a

as is befitting a festival such as this, to remind us that even though we will be fasting during the entire day from nightfall to nightfall, it is still a *festive* period, as we rejoice in our faith that our past sins will be erased on that very day and that our credit will be good once again.

And so there they sat, eating and drinking, Plimo at the head of the table all bedecked in his finest and feeling beside himself, in a *good* way, when this repulsive scrounger comes knocking in the middle of this most sacred feast. Plimo, being the pious and benevolent patron that he was, rose immediately from the comfort of his cushions, swung open the door, and brought the stranger a plate of delicacies and some bread, even some wine, and placed it on his front porch for the man to sit and eat there.

No sooner had Plimo sat back down at the table inside the house when he heard the strange stranger begin to snarl and grumble.

"So!!" the man yelled, "everyone sits on cushions inside the comfort of the house and I have to sit out here on this wooden bench?!"

Plimo rose up, went outside and invited the man inside and, because of his stench, seated him in a corner away from the dinner table. No sooner had Plimo rejoined his guests when he heard the beggar begin to snarl and grumble again.

"So!!" the man yelled, this time even louder, and foaming at the mouth, "everyone gets to sit together around the dinner table and I have to sit here in the corner all by my**self** like some kind of *reject*?!"

Plimo rose up again and escorted the stranger to the table, much to the disappointment of his guests who by now were trying not to inhale too deeply due to the stench of urine, smoke and mildew. The man sat down on one of Plimo's favorite cushions, sipped from his goblet, then spat-out the wine in disgust. Then he dipped his filth-caked hand into the shared soup bowl to retrieve a chunk of meat, tasted it, and spat that out too.

Plimo had about had it up to and beyond "here." He rose up out of his cushions, walked over to the man, seized him by the arm, and began shouting angrily into his mud-covered ears: "How dare you come into my home and insult me, my family, my guests, my mother-in-law's cooking!! I have been more than gener...."

The man, shocked by the assault, dropped his plate, and fell to the floor, unresponsive.

Plimo knelt by the man, checked his pulse, ordered a feather be held over his nostrils, and, it then dawned upon him like a meteor crashing down from the skies that the stranger was *dead*, that he'd caused a man to *die*!!!!!! -- and on the eve of *Yom Kippur* to *boot*!!! Plimo up and dashed to his bedchamber where he dropped to the floor and wept profusely. He could not believe it!! Here he was preparing to enter the holiest day of the year, the Day of **Atonement**! And he had lost his temper and *killed* a man!!! His entire life was ruined!! What was there to live for now!? How could he ever again celebrate Yom Ki....

His laments were suddenly interrupted by a gentle tap on his shoulder.

With great trepidation, Plimo turned around.

It was him. The beggar. The dead man. Except he wasn't dead, after all. Before Plimo could utter a sound, ask a question, express an emotion, the filthy, smelly, disheveled stranger began to shape-shift before his eyes, and within moments morphed into a beautiful, glowingly angelic being.

"But who…who…what…who are you?" Plimo could barely speak.

"I am *he*, the one you pray against daily, Plimo, the one in whose eyes you keep shooting imaginary arrows; the one you keep asking God to keep away from you and your family."

"You are **him**? The Satan? The Angel of Darkness? The Illusionist?"

"I am he."

"Why did you frighten me like this? You have no idea how terrified and hopeless and…I mean that was a horrific trick to pl…."

"Horrific, you say? Well, isn't that how you have thought of me all along? Isn't that the theme of your prayers about me? So what did you *expect*?"

"Well, what *should* I be praying about you?"

"Pray that God bless me in that the goodness he desires for his world be brought to its most optimal fruition by my working its opposite."

"But I thought that you…."

"That I am all about evil. Well, I will have you know that what I did to you tonight was a good thing, a precious gift, for until this moment you would have entered this holy of all days presuming you were righteous and sinless, when all along, festering inside of you, was the potential to blow up at some poor helpless hungry beggar and have him thrown feet first out of your home. Now, however, that dormant sin has been externalized, cut out of you like a boil removed from a diseased person, and you can enter Yom Kippur clean and whole, a truly remorseful penitent who has confessed what he might never have had the opportunity to confess about himself, having for so long veiled it comfortably beneath self-righteousness and in the guise of religious piety. It is my job to call your bluff, and so I did. And now your Yom Kippur will be the most beautiful and most sacred and most meaningful than ever it was."

And with that, The Illusionist flapped his wings and flew off into the realms of the Great Unknown. And Plimo lived happily ever after, and never again uttered so much as a single negative word in regard to The Illusionist, for he had never been so enlightened by anyone as he had by the Angel of Darkness.

And as for the trauma Plimo experienced from what he *thought* had happened but that actually *didn't* in the way he *thought* it did – well, it shape-shifted into a Living Goat and wandered into the desert in search of Aza'zel. For only Aza'zel can take back a memory and destroy the negatives.

Chapter Five

FLEEING IS BELIEVING

"All creatures of the sea," taught the ancient Hebrew masters, "are considered ritually pure, except for the Sea Dog (sea otter), because when it is troubled, it flees to the dry land."[66]

In other words, as my teacher explained it way way back when I was a sweet pure innocent student in Jerusalem: If you make something out of the skins of any creature of the sea, it does not absorb ritual impurities, and can therefore always be used as a ritual implement or vessel for sacred ceremony around people, places, or things that are in a state of ritual **im**purity -- except the skins of Sea Otters. Why?

Simply because under duress they head for the beach instead of the water. Under duress is when our **real** Self emerges, our convictions are put to the test, our bluff is called. Under duress we discover the truth of what a person or creature **truly** is about. Sea Otters presume to be creatures of the water, living in the water, traversing the oceans, but when push comes to shove, they head for dry land, thereby showing their true colors, so to speak -- that

---

[66] *Talmud Bav'li, Key'lim* 17:13

they are dry-land creatures, not water creatures. And as dry-land creatures, their skins absorb ritual impurities and cannot be used for sacred rituals around items or people in a state of ritual impurity.

I know. Right now you're going like *"Wha...?"* and others of you are tweeting to PETA, and yet others are lighting a match to the book, and the rest of you are taking a second look at the cover of this book to make sure it hadn't been switched on you. Please remember that these teachings do not advocate skinning animals. They originate in eras long before the introduction of clothes made of rayon, polyester, spandex, and other synthetic fibers. And if you were living back then, you'd probably be the first to skin a bear in the cold of winter without batting an eyelash. In fact, "Until the nineteenth century, cruelty to animals was nowhere illegal, except in Jewish law."[67]

So tighten your polyurethane belt and listen. Be patient. Allow me to explain. To quote from the 2011 film *Midnight in Paris*: "Pay attention, you might *loin* something."

Water, you see, is a veil. It conceals the mystery of Earth. And when Creator told Water to recede and **reveal** Earth,[68] the mystery of Earth emerged in all her glory, replete with living beings of innumerable varieties, from stone beings, sprouting beings, animal beings and finally **human** beings. Earth then represents mystery **un**veiled. Both realms, the realm of mystery **veiled** – Water – and that of mystery **revealed** – Earth – have their own keepers

---

[67] Sir Cecil Roth in *The Jewish Contribution to Civilization* [Macmillan, 1938], p. 343f

[68] Genesis 1:9

who thrive in those realms, respectively. Dolphins and tuna, for example, can only thrive in the realm of the veiled, while tigers and ducks can only thrive in the realm of the revealed. Sea Otters, on the other hand, can thrive in either, but when push comes to shove, they head for the realm of the revealed, implying thereby that they are not in essence creatures of the veil but of the **un**veiled, even though they spend **most** of their time in the **veiled**.

In my people's ancient ways, the idea of "purity" versus "impurity" has nothing at all to do with clean or dirty, as well-meaning translators of our ancient scriptures will have you believe. The original Hebraic words for either implies "clear" and "full," respectively. Impure, in other words – *tum'ah* -- implies a state of overload, wherein one is so full of some drama or trauma that there is no space for the restoration of equilibrium. Purification would then mean a ritual by which that restoration is enabled, as the word for purity – *taharah* – means "cleared." It's sort of like you're driving down the highway and your exit is coming up and there is no space in the exit lane for you to merge. And then someone in the exit lane backs off a tad, creating a cleared space for you to resume the flow of your journey. (You can tell I commute to work daily).

As long as I am stuck in a state of "impurity," my fullness affects my surroundings and everyone around me in one way or another, no less than does the sullenness of a grieving person influence the mood of those around them, as well as their immediate environment. How often have you said or heard someone remark "This place is depressing"? Or: "The air in here feels heavy." The potency of impurity and its far-reaching effects are indisputable.

Conversely, you might have at some point said or heard it said that "We need to clear the air," which, if it were spoken by a shaman, would be worded as "We need to purify the space."

You are most welcome to explain away all of this in scientific or psychological terms if that is your way, but as for me -- I am coming from my people's ancient and more aboriginal mindset. So, stay open and you will learn some important wisdom around living a meaningful life without purpose.

Not everything absorbs the energies of fullness, but among the things that do, is skin, whether yours or that of a Sea Otter. So, in modern terms of hygiene, when your skin has had contact with something wreaking of "fullness" you will not feel clear of that fullness until you've rinsed your skin, right? By fullness, I mean that your skin came in contact with something, the sense of which continued to linger in your consciousness thereafter and wouldn't go away until you "purified" yourself by washing-up. See what I mean? So, one way or another, the contact, the encounter, *filled* you, in that it prevented you from going on with the flow of your life, instead keeping you preoccupied with looking for a faucet and a bar of soap. Admit it or not, you now need to **clear out** what is **filling** you. So, perhaps now you can understand the concepts of ritual purity and impurity in aboriginal terms, and the rites of ceremonial cleansing so prevalent in ancient cultures and traditions.

Skin is a veil. It both protects what is inside *from* what is outside while also reflecting what is inside *to* the outside. It both conceals and reveals, concealing what you **look like** beneath it all, and revealing what you're **feeling** beneath it all. As such, it is therefore prone to the absorption of "fullness," of impurities, since in itself it is by nature quite full. Since it is by its very nature in constant contact with what is outside of it, it inevitably **absorbs** what is outside of it and picks up quite easily on any impurities lurking about in close proximity, and certainly by contact. Therefore, you will sometimes feel like your skin is "crawling" or get "goose bumps" even though no contact was made with anything, including geese, but your skin sensed something lurid enough to "fill you."

The skin of a dolphin or a catfish doesn't work in the same way as that of a giraffe or a lizard. Because dolphin and catfish are of the Realm of the Veil -- Water. Water does not absorb. Water **is** absorbed. Earth, on the other hand, **absorbs** but is not absorbed. Water cannot dissolve Earth. But Earth can dissolve Water. That which has been revealed can absorb that which once concealed it. That which conceals cannot absorb that which it has revealed. We live by virtue of our absorption of that from which we emerged, but that from which we emerged does not live by absorbing that which emerged from it any more than can a mother return a newborn into her womb.

So, going back to the original teaching: if you make something out of the skins of any creature of the sea, it does not absorb ritual impurities, and can therefore always be used as a ritual implement or vessel for sacred ceremony around people, places, or things that are in a state of ritual **im**purity -- except the skins of sea otters. Why? Because under duress they head for the beach instead of the water, which demonstrates that they are not creatures belonging in *essence* to the realm of the concealed but to the realm of the revealed.

Likewise, the truth of a person's selfhood, the veracity of their essence, is brought out by their reaction under duress. Sort of like another Talmudic dictum: "We know a person by their *ko's, kees,* and *ka'as* (literally: goblet, pocket, and temper), by how they react when inebriated, when under financial strain, and in the heat of conflict.[69]

The sea otter, taught Efraim Zeitchik, one of my early teachers, is truly a creature of the waters, spends most of its time in the waters, is happiest in the waters, flourishes in and is nourished by the sea. Yet, in moments of trouble, it leaves all that it craves and yearns for most, and opts for the alien habitat of dry land. And likewise, so do we. We yearn for, crave, dabble in, seek, embrace, all that is good and holy and spiritual; bask ourselves in all that is positive and sacred and inspirational; swim in the seas of love and charity and mercy and compassion and peace; embrace all that is right and proper and ethical. But when we are suddenly pushed into a corner...we leave this beautiful vast sea of all these soul-nourishing qualities and attributes of ennoblement, and leap into a realm that is otherwise alien to us, a realm of fury, violence, jealousy, hate, judgment, cruelty, and conflict.[70]

To be a vessel that will not take on the "impurities" of life, the antithesis to our personal truths, we need to examine within and work at our behavioral qualities, our relationships with our loved ones at home, to make sure

---

[69] *Talmud Bav'li, Eruvin* 65b

[70] *To'rat Ha'Nefesh*, p. 225

we are what we're cracked up to be, and that under strain we will not transmute into a whole other creature.

Noticing how we respond to stressful situations and making the effort to clear out that which overwhelms us in the moment is an important practice toward living a meaningful life. It can improve our relationships, our well-being, our health, and maybe even the condition of our world.

Chapter Six

THE TAO OF HAVING

There is this strange concept in ancient Jewish wisdom: You cannot fill a vessel that is empty. Only if it's got something in it -- **any**thing. To receive Blessing you need a "Vessel capable of **grasping** Blessing," the ancients insisted, and, in fact, "Less grasps More."[71] This seems puzzling on the surface of it because why else would I be in need of Blessing if I weren't running on empty? It is precisely because I am **lacking** that I am in **need**!

Let me tell you a story.

About 2800 years ago, there was a great prophet named Elisha. He was the foremost disciple of the famous prophet Elijah, and he was a seasoned miracle-worker, a real true-blue shaman. One day, Elisha is sitting surrounded by hundreds of people who have come to hear him teach when a local baker arrives and gifts the prophet with a couple of freshly-baked loaves. Elisha accepts the bread, thanks the man and then instructs his helper to share the bread with everyone. The helper looks around at the several hundred people gathered around the prophet and says, "No way. There are only like twenty loaves here and

---

[71] *Midrash Bereisheet Rabbah 5:7*

more than a hundred mouths." Elisha again insists that the loaves be shared with *everyone*, and, in fact, he assures his aide, there will even be **left**overs! So, the helper goes around handing out the bread, and lo and behold the loaves multiply and keep multiplying until everyone in the crowd has been fed, and there is plenty left over as well.[72]

So, Elisha was that kind of guy.

Well, one day, a widow who had fallen on very hard times came to Elisha to seek his help. She had lost everything, was very poor, and in deep debt, to the point that she was going to have to offer her sons as indentured servants unless some miracle occurred soon. Elisha then asked her "What do you have in your home?" She says, "I have nothing in my home other than a teeny-tiny drop of oil." Says Elisha, "Go to your neighbors and borrow from them as many empty pots and pans as you can. Then go home, shut the door behind you, and pour that teeny-tiny drop of oil into all the vessels." The woman went to her neighbors and with the help of her sons schlepped dozens of empty containers of all sorts to her home, then went inside, shut the door behind her, and began filling all of them with oil as her teeny-tiny drop of oil miraculously swelled into gallons and gallons until she ran out of vessels. Elisha then instructed her to sell the oil, which she did, and soon she recouped financially and lived happily ever after.[73]

The ancient mystics taught us that Blessing is drawn from beyond us and from within us simultaneously; from Above and by what we **already** possess if we cherish the

---

[72] Second Kings, 4:42-44
[73] Second Kings, 4:1-7

gift of what we already **have**. When we cherish what we **do** have, no matter how little of it we own, the appreciation itself is potent enough to draw **further** blessing from the Root of **all** Blessing. This is why, when that poverty-stricken woman came to Elisha seeking his help, he didn't ask her what it was that she **lacked**. Rather, he asked her what it was that she **had**, that she cherished already **having**. Her reply sounded pathetic: "I have nothing in the house. Well, I **do** have a smidgen of oil" – which the second-century sage, Rav Yehudah, postulated was "just enough to spread across the tip of her finger." Elisha's reply, Rav Yehudah continues, was: "Oh! You have **consoled** me. I was worried you might have felt like you had nothing at **all**. But what you acknowledge that you **do** have is more than enough to draw Blessing from Above."[74] In other words, you took the time and effort to look beyond the obvious scenario of your situation to uncover the hidden, the blessings in your life that were overlooked, overshadowed by your problems.

The woman **could** have said, "I have nothing whatsoever." Because what is a smidgen of oil? But since she demonstrated her awareness of how even so little can be precious enough to be deemed a blessing to **some** degree – it sufficed to draw down **further** blessings of **further** degrees, enough to fill **all** of the pots and pans that she had borrowed from her neighbors.

Great teaching. In order to invite more of what you need, you must first come to grips with what you already have, even if it's just the shirt off your back, or your health, or enough of your health to move around, and so on.

---

74 Zohar, Vol. 1, folio 88a

Even if you have absolutely nothing at all but **peace**, it's a good start, "for there is no greater vessel capable of grasping Blessing than Peace."[75] It's like the Kabbalistic take on Creation, that the fledgling primeval universe was completely empty, and therefore when the Light of Creation entered it, it exploded, it shattered, because it was not a "Vessel capable of grasping Blessing" – having nothing within it. Shattered, it became filled with the sparks of the very same Light of Creation that it failed to contain, and thus, by becoming filled with **something**, even if only the debris of the implosion, it became a vessel capable of receiving the subsequent unfolding of existence as we have come to know it. (Remind you of the "Big Bang" theory?)

Blessing is primarily drawn not by virtue of what is obvious to us that we **have**, but of what is **not** obvious to us that we have.[76] What is conspicuous to us, is in that moment measurable as large, small, worth five dollars, worth three dollars, worth a buck-fifty, great, not so great, etc. On the other hand, taught the 16th-century Judah Loew of Prague, what we have that is **not** right off obvious to us is in the realm of the **im**measurable and draws Blessing because Blessing is **im**measurable as it emanates from the realm of the **In**finite as opposed to the Finite, "For the eye casts boundaries and limitations, whereas Blessings are without either."[77]

This is an exercise that requires us to look deep inside our life situations, to seek out what gifts we have

[75] *Midrash Bamid'bar Rabbah* 21:1

[76] *Talmud Bav'li, Baba Kama* 42a

[77] Maharal in *Chidushei Aggadot*, Vol. 3, folio 21

been in possession of all along but have been oblivious to all this time. (Remember the camel story?) This takes effort; this takes introspection. "The Blessing Flow from **Above**," taught the 16th-century mystic Menachem Azariah de Fano, "comes to us in strengths and quantities commensurate with our desires and efforts to draw it from **Below**. This is akin to breast milk, abundant and ready to flow forth, but dependent upon how determined the infant is in suckling."[78]

The widow in the story of Elisha did not stop at declaring that she had nothing in the house. She stayed with the question, examined deeply her situation to see if there was anything of any value in the house, and remembered that there was a teeny-tiny drop of something worth being thankful for.

Like the ancient teaching goes: "Before you ask God for what you lack, thank God for what you have."[79]

---

[78] *Kitzur Sefer Yo'nat Ilem*, No. 122

[79] *Midrash Devarim Rabbah* 2:1

Chapter Seven

HITHER, OR THITHER?

Listen. There is a 2,000-year-old teaching that goes something like this: When a woman and a man prepare to make love, God calls on the Angel of Pregnancy, who is called *Lie'lah* – literally: "Night" -- and says: "Tonight this one and that one are going to conceive. Go down there and make certain the seed becomes endowed with the potential to realize 365 organs, and then bring it to me."

Once the ovum is fertilized, it is seized by *Lie'lah* and brought before God. God then asks the angel in charge of souls to summon a particular soul from out of the Garden of Eden (Paradise), and says to it: "Hello, Soul. I would like you to enter this seed." The soul protests: "What!? But I **like** it here. I have loved it here from the very moment you first created me. Why would you want to remove me from this very sacred place and jam me into that repulsive yukky gooey glob that has come about from an act so thoroughly physical and – at least from my perspective – *obscene*!!? I am holy and pure and spiritual, and yet you want me to merge with that…that **slimy** thing?" To which God responds: "The world I wish to send you to is far more beautiful than the one you have been living in all this time, and it is for that slimy 'thing' that I created you in the first place, so get your ass in there and don't give me any more guff."[80]

A powerful teaching. This world, with all of its ups and downs and lefts and rights, goods and evils, pains and joys, yuks and yums – is hyped up to be a better place than the Spirit World from which everything originated, even more beautiful than Paradise itself!! This is so contrary a teaching to everything most of us have been taught, antithetical to everything we believe, a slap in the face of everything we've strived for!

What?! You mean to tell us that all these years of striving and struggling, rising and falling for the purpose of achieving spiritual awareness, is for naught? That all along we should have been focusing our awareness on this messed-up mundane inane profane vain and insane *earthly* life? What about all those teachings about spirituality? Spiritual consciousness? Spiritual this and spiritual that? How can the holy sages of yore be telling us that in God's opinion the world of the here-and-now is a far better place than the holy, pure, saintly sacred angelic realms of the **spirit** world? Of the Garden of **Eden**, no less.

I am perplexed.

I have to admit, that although I have been studying and teaching the perplexing lessons of my people's ancient wisdom now for close to fifty years, I still can't get used to it and am shocked every time. I am convinced that much of Judaism is what Tibetan Buddhism refers to as *drub'nyon*, or "Crazy Wisdom."

So, I went to the ancient masters for some explanation.

---

[80] *Midrash Tanchuma, P'kudei*, Chapter 3

And here is what the second-century Rav Ya'akov said: "More beautiful is one moment of personal transformation and doing good deeds in **this** world than an eternity in the World to Come; and more beautiful is one moment of bliss in the World to **Come** than an eternity of bliss in **this** world."[81]

Thank you. That was very helpful. Now I am even more confused.

So I visited the 16th-century mystic and shaman par-excellence Judah Loew of Prague (known also as the MAHARAL), famed creator of the legendary clay creature known as *The Golem*,[82] and asked him to clarify.

"You cannot change anything about yourself in the hereafter," he said, gathering a clump of virgin mud from the Moldau River and fashioning the image of a man. "You cannot do any personal transformation work in the Garden of Eden, he continued, in the Spirit World. In Paradise. Only **here**. Here is where you become dynamic. Here is where you flow, flux, flex and germinate. Not there. **Here**. In **this** world. In the Spirit World you simply are what you have become while you meandered about in **this** lifetime. In the hereafter you cannot execute the actual **becoming**, the infinite possibilities of transformation with which you are endowed. This only happens here, in **this** world, in the world of change, in the realm of instability, in the cauldron of relativity, in the arena of opportunity, in the gauntlet of challenge. This is the **happening** place – indeed a far more beautiful

---

[81] *Mishnah, Avot* 4:17

[82] Which you can read all about in my out-of-print classic: *The Golem of Prague* (Judaica Press, NY: 1980).

place to be, in contrast to the static, boring realm of spirit where you may fly around and shape-shift all you want and bask in the much-talked-about 'Divine Light' but you cannot change who or what you are in essence, let alone revel in any of it. All transformative work happens here. Only **here**. So do the work **here**. Don't wait to die, because over there you remain as you have become and can become no more than what you are. Here, however, you have moment to moment the opportunity, the challenge, to become **more** than what you are – or less, of course.

"So what the earlier master, Yaakov, was implying is, that if you haven't been here yet, this is a far more favorable place to relocate than the spirit realms in which you originate. And, conversely, if you **have** been here or are **still** here, let me assure you that in contrast to this place, a single moment in the World to Come yields far more bliss than a lifetime of bliss in **this** world."[83]

And if you think about it, First Human **had** to leave Paradise because how could they appreciate Paradise when they had not yet experienced its opposite? Not having known pain, they could not yet know pleasure. Not knowing sadness, they could not yet know joy. Not knowing anxiety, they could not yet know tranquility.

Bottom line, whether you believe in the spirit world, the world to come, the hereafter, life before life and life after death – or not – the lesson is important. Being here gifts us with unparalleled opportunity, infinite possibility, and a wealth of chance to change, alter, transform, improve, or

---

[83] *Derech Chayyim* on *Mishnah, Avot* 4:17

vice-versa. That alone makes this world, this lifetime, its foibles and troubles notwithstanding, a far better place to be – or, more to the point – to **become**.

So, welcome to the Garden of Paradox.

Enjoy your stay.

Chapter Eight

LIMBO

A quote from the Torah: "You shall not follow in the ways of the Land of Egypt where you were living, and you shall not follow in the ways of the Land of Canaan where I am bringing you."[84] In other words, the Israelites of the Exodus period some 3,400 years ago were warned against emulating the ways of Egypt, the only place they'd ever known, and also against learning from the ways of Canaan, the ancestral homeland to which they were returning after several centuries of absence. Pretty profound, when you think about it. What I have known in the past and what I endeavor to learn in the future is rendered moot and invalid in the moment, and I am left without any footing, neither a platform from which to leap nor ground upon which to land.

When the Israelites left Egypt back then, they were instructed to create a ritual kind of bread we to this day call "*matzoh*."[85] Matzoh consists of absolutely nothing other than Water and Earth (flour), the Alpha and Omega

---

[84] Leviticus 18:3
[85] Exodus 12:15

of Genesis. In the beginning there was water.[86] In the end there was earth.[87] And in between is the Bread of Limbo, known as "*matzoh*," related to the Hebrew word for "Discovery" (*matzi'a*).

What are we to do, as we meander about between the mystery that is our origin and the mystery that is our destiny? What are we to discover as we emerge from the fertile Sea of Reeds onto the barrenness of wilderness? The instruction that Moses channeled from God continues: "Rather, my guidance shall you follow, and my injunctions shall you observe...which, if a person follows and tends to, they will **live** through them."[88]

Cool. So, we're supposed to let go of what we've learned and steer clear of any lessons that are destined to come our way, and instead do, learn, observe, exactly **what**?

This: "Don't ever enter the mystery of another, even those close to you. None of you may ever approach your father to uncover his mystery, nor your mother to uncover **her** mystery; she is your mother, so don't expose her mystery. Do not reveal the mystery of the wife of your father, she is your father's mystery. Do not uncover the mystery of your sister, whether daughter of your father or daughter of your mother, and whether she was born within the family structure or outside the family structure; you may not expose their mysteries."[89]

All we need to know in the Now, in the moment between moments, in our limbo sojourn in the desolate wilderness between Egypt and Canaan, between our

---

[86] Genesis 1:2

[87] Genesis 1:9

[88] Leviticus 18:4-5

[89] Leviticus 18:6-9 and on

yesterday and our tomorrow, is simply this: try not to uncover what is concealed. Do not presume, judge, assume, and guess meanings that are veiled by the day-to-day camouflage of life. We need rather to **revere** mystery, not endeavor to expose her.

Father and Mother represent our past, where we came from, our Egypt. Sister represents our present, our life as it rolls alongside us, whether it is a life defined by that part of our past that we relate to our father's influence or a life defined by that part of our past that we relate to our mother's influence; whether our life as it has come to be defined by our home upbringing or our life as it has come to be defined by external influences.

Like the 18th-century Reb Zusia of Hanipol interpreted God's revelatory oration to Abraham: "Go to yourself, away from your land, away from your birth place, away from the house of your father, to the land that I will show you'...[90] This implies the following: 'Away from your land' -- get away from the dimness caused by the ways in which you have been acculturated in your country of origin; 'away from your birth place' -- get away from the dimness caused by some of the ways in which you may have been influenced by your mother; 'away from your father's house' -- get away from the dimness caused by some of the ways in which you may have been influenced by your father; 'to the land that I will show you' -- for only THEN will you be able to see that which is waiting to be revealed to you."

The message is very clear: Do not allow yourself to slip-slide into the quagmire of what has come before you,

---

[90] Genesis 12:1

and likewise do not obsess yourself with getting to where you are heading. Rather, grab some *matzoh*, the bread of the Exodus, comprised simply of flour and water, and return to the awareness of the mystery that you yourself embody rather than clamoring to uncover the mystery of all else that surrounds you.

Listen to this. The ancient teachers, in discussing the above quotations from the Torah, offer us this challenging commentary: "The ways of Egypt that the Israelites were forbidden to follow were actually inspired by the Israelites themselves; the ways of Canaan that the Israelites were forbidden to follow were, too, actually inspired by the Israelites themselves."[91]

Pretty cool, no? The early masters are proposing that the very practices of Egypt and Canaan that we were instructed not to emulate were the very practices we ourselves inspired in Egypt during our sojourn there, and in Canaan when we arrived there. Judaism 101. A tradition of paradox and perplexity.

What, pray tell, did we inspire within or contribute to the ancient Egyptian culture during our sojourn there that could have turned out so terrible that we were forbidden from taking it with us when we left? And more perplexing, what influence could we possibly have had on the culture of Canaan before we'd even **arrived** there, and so much so that we were forewarned ahead of time not to **continue** it even though we hadn't **begun**!?

One of the many things we mortals are shy about admitting is that we are creatures of interruption. We are – in science fiction terms – "space invaders." The moment

---

[91] *Midrash Sif'ri, Vayik'ra* 18:3

I set foot into the space of another, I upset the balance of the ingredients that constitute their life flow. This is true even in any relationship, including our well-meaning institution of marriage. Neither party to an encounter of any sort, whether business or romantic, is the same as they were prior to the relationship. When we engage one another, we each bring our glitter and our litter to the purity of each other's individuality and self-essence and end up either fostering or contaminating that purity. Wise is the teaching of the second-century master, Akiva ben Yosef: "A man should never enter his home without first announcing his arrival, lest he disrupt the private flow of those inside the home."[92] Only after studying this maxim in my teens did I finally understand why my father always – and I mean **always** – whistled a familiar note, as if it were some sort of signal, before he approached the front door on his return from work. My mother's face would then light up, and we kids would scurry to the door with bated breath.

Ever since the first human encountered his and her Other, both were transformed into something different than what they were prior. Both had their personal equilibrium turned upside down and inside out. "The Woman you set me up with gave me of the tree, and so I ended up eating [the Forbidden Fruit]," pleaded First Man. "The Serpent *tricked* me!" pleaded First Woman.[93] In other words, each of us is predisposed to organ rejection whenever a transplant occurs, whether it's a heart, a liver, a kidney, or another person.

---

[92] *Talmud Bav'li, Pesachim* 112a and *Niddah* 16b
[93] Genesis 3:12-13

When we enter the arena of relationship, we are basically grafting two different species of beings onto one another. Sometimes it takes, sometimes it doesn't, but one way or another the grafting itself creates a conglomerate which becomes something other than the individual components that comprise it – for better, or for worse. Therefore, a healthy relationship is one in which both parties respect each other's right to their idiosyncrasies and eccentricities and quirks not only at the outset but through**out** the course of the relationship. Unsuccessful relationships, on the other hand, result from one or both parties being dead-set on re-creating the other in their image. In other words, the grafting does not take, does not morph into an organic coexistence. Rather, it is duct-taped.

Another scenario in the universe of interrelating and space invading is one in which the transplant takes just fine at first, but then causes problems down the line due to contraindicative circumstances, meaning that the bonding triggers -- in either or both parties to the relationship -- reactions that gradually poison rather than foster their coexistence. This is sort of like taking medication prescribed for a particular ailment which then causes adverse side-effects later on. So, while the drug is working just fine in curing the ailment for which it was prescribed, it results in awakening a whole other set of complications **else**where in the body a year or three later.

In either of the scenarios, the issue, again, is that no one is actually made for anyone else. Marriages are *not* made in heaven. They are made right here on Planet Earth through lots of roller-coasting. They are made by our endeavors to work toward meaning as opposed to aiming for purpose. If my purpose is to turn you into me, or to preserve the template of our relationship even as its contents are crumbling, our relationship will sail aimlessly farther and farther out into the Sea of Oblivion. If I work at bringing **meaning** to the relationship by doing my part in furthering – rather than changing – the uniqueness of who you are, and making you breakfast even when you don't ask me, and bringing you flowers even if there is no occasion looming in the Hallmark horizon, then our relationship will sail into the Sea of Bliss. Purpose is goal-oriented; meaning is moment-oriented. Purpose is designed; meaning is spontaneous.

In the words of the 18th-century Mendl of Kotzk: "If you are you because I am I, and I am I because you are you, then I am not I and you are not you. But if I am I because I am I, and you are you because you are you, then you are you and I am I."

What we brought to our relationship with ancient Egypt at first **took**,[94] as they say, but over time turned out to be contraindicated, resulting in complications that proved unwholesome,[95] and so we were instructed when we left not to take that blend with us. It is no wonder that in the original Hebraic vernacular, the exodus of the Israelites from their centuries-old sojourn in Egypt is described as the "***extrication*** of one people from within the ***bowels*** of another."[96] Not an exodus but an *extrication*, a kind of *surgical removal* – medically indicated.

---

[94] Genesis 47:1-7 and Exodus 1:7

[95] Exodus 1:8-14

[96] Deuteronomy 4:34

Truth be told, we don't mix well. We wouldn't have fared any better, in other words, trying to blend in with the Canaanites any more than we failed in blending in with the Egyptians. We were a people onto ourselves. And this is true in regard to each of us. We don't blend well, neither where we come from, nor where we're headed. Because when we try to blend, we are operating in Purpose Mode, the purpose being to *blend*. When we **don't** try to blend but focus on our own uniqueness as individuals, or as a culture, then we foster meaning, and the blend, if it is meant to be, will happen and wholesomely so. Just like in any good solid relationship. If you go out on a date with the purpose of making it happen, chances are it won't, and your date may have to get a restraining order. If you make your date a meaningful one, chances are it might lead to something – and meaningfully so.

The walk we were instructed 3,400 years ago was very simple: Honor the mystery of the other, rather than endeavor to uncover it. Meaning, versus purpose. Purpose invites judgment; meaning invites appreciation. If someone is nicer than you, laud them for it; if someone is more beautiful than you, praise them for it; if someone is so radically different from you, celebrate them. Don't try to strip them of their mystery and presume to know their Truth, and don't be too quick to judge their superior qualities as false or shallow. Respect the awesomeness of wonder rather than dilute it with your obsession of decoding what is encrypted.

The Torah, wrote Abraham Joshua Heschel, "is primarily divine **ways**, rather than divine **laws**."[97] Moses,

---

[97] *God in Search of Man* (Schocken Books), p. 288

after all, did not ask God to teach him God's "laws" but rather God's "ways."[98] Those "ways" are to be found neither in Egypt where we grew up nor in Canaan where we settled down. They are rather to be found in Limbo Land, in the desert, in the **act** of the Exodus rather than in the **climax** of the Exodus, in the "going **out** from the Land of Egypt" rather than in the "arriving **in** the Land of Canaan." There, somewhere between our Genesis and our Nemesis, between our birth and our death, there we walk, there we listen, there we see, and there we learn. And there we free ourselves of spiritual and emotional atrophy. And there we not only open our eyes but more importantly we "**lift**" our eyes and see from a distance; behold the bigger picture.[99]

It is interesting that the original word for Passover, *PeSaKH* -- implies the capacity to leap, to spring, to jump, to be limber and free, and yet at the same time it also can read as *PeeSayaKH*, which means lame, incapacitated, immobilized, barely hobbling along. This is the price of conscientious living. As the ancestral father Jacob quickly learned after a successful night-long conflict-resolution fray with an angel. Successful, yes, but he walked away from the scuffle with a chronic limp.[100]

If you dare to leap above and beyond the ways in which you are accustomed to seeing the world around you, and to see it differently each moment, be prepared also to sprain an ankle or two and hobble for a while. If you wish to pursue the mystery of all that surrounds you,

---

[98] Exodus 33:13
[99] Genesis 22:4
[100] Genesis 32:26 and 32

let go of it; release your grip from what you have been staunchly holding on to and refrain from reaching for the next handle and allow yourself to drop into the chasm of mystery between water and earth, between your Genesis and your Nemesis, your yesterday and your tomorrow. **There** lies the *Matzoh*, **there** the mystery allows itself to be Discovered; **there** the veil drops and the eyes are lifted above and beyond to see what is otherwise hidden. There, you may also sprain an ankle when you land or twist a knee on impact, but you will never hit rock bottom.

Yes, there is a price on attempting to walk a meaningful life, with or without purpose, but it is a price well worth paying for the deep inner bliss of feeling more alive than ever.[101] "A human being," wrote Abraham Joshua Heschel, "must be valued by how many times he was able to see the world from a new perspective."[102]

---

[101] Leviticus 18:5
[102] *Moral Grandeur and Spiritual Audacity,* p. 20

Chapter Nine

BUZZARD

Listen. There is an eagle-like bird my people are forbidden to eat.[103] It is a species of desert vulture known as *Roh'chom*, which is Hebrew for "compassion," because "when a *Roh'chom* flies overhead, it is an omen for heavenly compassion."[104] Compassion is something you'd like to **have**, not **eat**. In later times, we called it a *Sh'rak'rak* because "rak rak" is the sound it makes when it sings. Moreover, taught the second-century Bibi bar Abaye,[105] "If ever a *Roh'chom* would chance to alight upon the earth and sing, it is a sign that the Messiah has come, as is written, '*Esh'rekah* [I shall shriek] onto them and gather them, for I have redeemed them.'"[106]

Pretty wild. Basically, when this buzzard will one day swoop down from the skies above and alight upon the earth and go "rak rak", it means redemption from all of our struggles is at hand. But a buzzard? Why not, say, a hummingbird, or a canary, or a colorful macaw, or any

---

[103] Leviticus 11:18

[104] *Talmud Bav'li, Chulin* 63a

[105] *Talmud Bav'li, Chulin* 63a

[106] Zechariah 10:8

one of myriad species of nice, sweet gorgeous birds **other** than the one most notorious for feeding on dying animals?

The first mention of buzzard in my people's sacred story, the Torah, appears in the account around our ancestor Abraham's covenantal vision[107] which takes place during a three-day vision quest some 4,000 years ago. On the first day, he gathers a heifer, a goat, a ram, a turtle-dove and a young dove. He splits in half the heifer, the goat, the ram, and the turtle-dove, but not the young dove, at which point a Spirit Fire whooshes through the middle, in between the animal halves. He is then visited by an *a'yeet*, a species of buzzard. The buzzard gifts Abraham with the Breath of Life taken from the last breath of the dying, with which Abraham then restores the **parted** animals back to life.[108]

On the **second** day of this shamanic journey, Abraham is enveloped in a spirit of darkness and goes into a deep trance in which Creator informs him that his descendants are destined to become strangers in a foreign land for a period of four hundred cycles, after which they will be redeemed, and after which they will exit their struggles with great bounty and return to their homeland. On the **third** day, Abraham awakens from the trance and sees the remnants of the Spirit Fire that had passed earlier between the carcasses. In other words, it had not been a dream but it had actually happened in real life, real-time.

Yes, I know. This version of the story is not the way you read it in the English translations of the Hebraic

---

[107] Genesis 15:9-14

[108] 11th-century Rabbi Shlomo Yitzchaki [Rashi]; 19th-century Rabbi Meir leibush in *Mal'bim ahl HaTorah* on Genesis 15:11

Scriptures. That is the flaw in available translations that I have been ranting about for decades.

It is interesting to note that during the course of Abraham's three-day vision quest, all three dramatic experiences -- the splitting and restoration of the animal parts, the prophecy about his descendants, and the real-time evidence of the Spirit Fire – occur at nightfall.[109] What is even more fascinating is that nightfall in ancient Hebrew is *bo ha'shemesh* "**coming** of the Sun"[110] when one would suppose it ought to be "**going** of the Sun." I mean, how would it sound to you if I told you that I will see you later tonight when the Sun comes?

Obviously, as with so much else in the ancient language of my people, there is a deep deep lesson itching to emerge here. Simply put, the ancient Hebrew vocabulary has no such word as "Sunset" or "Sundown." Because the Sun never goes down. It is always **coming**. You just have to wait out the night, but ultimately the Sun will be coming, always coming, never going, never setting, and never leaving. It is this mindset that has helped my people to last as long as they have. Regardless of how long and endless seemed the night, we always believed, always knew, that daylight is approaching. And this is why we are always directing ourselves toward the East. Not because Jerusalem is east of wherever we are. That's too simplistic. I mean, it's also west of wherever we are. I mean, what if I'm living **east** of Jerusalem? Or to the north or south of it? No, we face East because we are always waiting for the Sun

---

[109] Genesis 15:5, 12 and 17

[110] For example, Genesis 28:11, Exodus 17:12 and 22:25, Leviticus 22:7, Psalms 50:1 and 113:3, Ecclesiastes 1:5, Malachi 1:11, etc., etc., etc.

to come, for newness to break forth, for light to emerge from out of the darkness. And, as the prophet Isaiah told us some 2,700 years ago, the *a'yeet*, that very same buzzard that visited Abraham during his vision quest and by whose breath he resurrected the halved animals, "is summoned from the East,"[111] from the place of new beginnings, the place of shining, and the place of hope. As a people, this has been our motto throughout our history: "They can take away my sustenance (heifer), my power (ram), my tenacity (goat), even my old hope (turtle-dove), but they cannot take away my ever-**renewing** hope (young dove)."

This is why Abraham did not split in half the young dove, the bird that symbolizes fresh hope, the bird that brought to Noah a twig from an olive branch to restore hope to a world gone under (no reference to Australia intended).[112] Why particularly a **young** dove? Because old hope grows stale after a while. It becomes routine. My people is still praying for the opportunity to return to our homeland when the homeland is now again available and waiting for **us** to return. Old hopes become stale when they put us to sleep and prevent us from recognizing the realization of those hopes when it happens. We need **new** hope, or at least **renewed** hope.

So, yeah, the Messianic happening being announced by a buzzard makes all the sense in the world. She carries the life breath of struggle. And when she will alight from the heavens and perch herself upon the earth to restore within us what has become fragmented, we will know that the messianic hope is being realized. She will perform

[111] Isaiah 46:11

[112] Genesis 8:11

this restoration by singing her song with the very breath of struggle that we had sighed in each of those moments of challenge in our lives, of hardship.

As Moses once prayed: "Gladden us commensurate with the days of our misfortunes, those many years during which we witnessed misfortune."[113] For, when the Sun comes, all of our grief will be transformed into dance,[114] our weeping into song,[115] and every sigh you ever breathed will be breathed back into you, albeit as a breath of renewed life and joy. And we will become one with the one who is "Only," or -- as the Hebrew word for "only" sounds -- "*rak*."

---

[113] Psalms 90:15

[114] Psalms 30:12

[115] Psalms 126:5

Chapter Ten

MIRIAM'S CURE

> All rivers, when they flow across the
> earth, they are sweet, blessed, and
> wholesome, and they bring pleasure
> to the world. Once they merge with
> the sea, however, they lose their
> goodness and turn bitter, and bring
> no pleasure to the world.[116]

Our gifts, our talents, our powers, they flow across our
lives like rivers nourishing the earth. Yet, there are times
and circumstances when what we deem to be our purpose,
our work here, sours on us, loses its potency, sheds its effect
on the world around us, and is washed into the vastness of
Oblivion. So easily can the very thing we feel empowered
by become the very thing that **dis**empowers us. If we keep
our efforts in the world directed and focused, it remains
sweet and wholesome; if we allow it to become diluted by
stress and routine, it becomes something else, exiled from
our deep soul-self, and rendered inauthentic to us as well
as to those around us.

---

[116] *Midrash Pirkei D'Rebbe Eliezer*, Ch. 8

The metaphor of the sea is about obscurity, unconscious rote living with no "land" in the horizon, no sense of direction or point of reference. This often happens to us by default when we are involved daily, hourly, in the dynamics of our work or our relationships, whether with intimate partners or childrearing. There is no welcome shout of "Land Ho!!", only the ongoing "same-old, same-old" float across the vast sea of endless time. Every day the same routine, every day the same face or faces, the same challenges, the same problems to plow through, the same situations to negotiate, the same cause and effect, the same reactions, the same demands of our time, our energy, our very soul.

Floating about on a shredding life-raft, we find ourselves at the mercy of the sea and its unpredictable waves or moods; we have by then forgotten something very important... the joy and celebration we felt when the child or children first came into our lives, or when we first encountered our significant other or dog. We have by then forgotten the potency of our commitment to them, to loving, to building, to deepening our relationship. We have by then forgotten that we once flowed like the rapids of the Colorado River, snaking our way through any circumstance, any obstacle, nurturing self and other along the way with sweetness, with bliss, with beauty, with love, and with sacrifice. By then we have forgotten all this and find ourselves instead meandering along like debris from a sunken ship being cast about by the waves of *Whatever.*

This is what happened to my ancestors when they were slaves for several centuries in ancient Egypt. They lost their fervor, their passion, their lust, and resigned to just drift aimlessly across the vast sea of existence with neither sail nor compass: dead to self and other.

Until Miriam the Prophetess, sister of Moses and Aaron, in a moment of epiphany shattered the rote, emerged from the Sea of the Great Void, and sounded the rhythm of her drum, shattering the cadence of unconscious existence and restoring the tempo of aliveness and passion. Had she not done this, Moses would have crossed the Sea of Reeds with a handful instead of multitudes. Miriam, the ancients tell us, resurrected the people's long-dead passion, the passion they once knew for one another, the passion that had long since been swept into the sea and drowned.[117] Miriam, in other words, was the first to "split the sea" where it counted most. If the Sea of Reeds had not been split by Moses, my ancestors would have died a physical death. If the Sea of **Oblivion** had not been split by Miriam they would have died a spiritual and emotional death.

Later, when Moses was instructed to make the sacred copper basin for ritual cleansing, God told him it had to be constructed exclusively out of the very copper mirrors that the **women** had donated because these mirrors in particular had become sacred by virtue of having been used by these women to restore passion to their men.[118]

What an important lesson for us all. When we start to feel that what was once *Wow!!* has become *Ho-Hum...*, we need to realize that our Colorado is emptying into the Gulf. It is then that we have to pull ourselves back out of the undertow of the Sea of Oblivion and restore the

[117] *Talmud Bav'li, Sotah* 12b
[118] Exodus 38:8; *Midrash Tanchuma, P'koo'dey*, No. 9

passion we once knew when we were rivers and rapids; to look again at our partners as if it were the first time, to look at our children as they nag us for this and that and remember the miracle of their Genesis in our lives, to look at our work and remember how excited we were to get our first paycheck; to remember Miriam's magical drum and brazen resolve; to remember the wise words of Solomon some 3,000 years ago: "All the rivers journey to the sea, and yet the sea is never filled; back to the place where the rivers walk, there they return to walk again."[119]

Don't forget the oars.

---

[119] *Kohelet* 1:7

Chapter Eleven

URGENCY

The second-century master, Tar'fon, was best known for his practical aphorisms, one of the most famous being: "The work is not upon you to finish; nor are you exempt from trying."[120]

This lesson appears to discourage urgency, the desperation we often experience around completing something, fixing something, achieving, accomplishing. We would love to just make everything okay in this world, and we suffer severe disappointment in our failure to do so. No matter how many peace protests we attend, no matter how many petitions we sign, no matter how many rallies for this or that or the other...things just don't seem to ever change that much, or make a difference. After a while, it gets tiring and we start to wear down, even throw up our arms, stop trying altogether, and automatically delete those pesky emails that beckon to be forwarded to others.

And so, Tar'fon's adage comes along and soothes our dampened spirits, reminding us to cool-out our urgency, our drive to complete, to accomplish -- that the task is

---

[120] *Mishnah, Avo't* 2:16

not upon us to finish, rather it is upon us to keep trying anyhow. This life is not so much about accomplishment as it is about effort, he stressed. "In accordance with the degree of the effort," echoed Ben Hei'hei, one of Tar'fon's contemporaries, "is the degree of the reward."[121]

What puzzles me regarding Tar'fon's teaching about stepping back from urgency is an earlier teaching of his: "The day is short, the work is great, the laborers are lazy, the remuneration is magnanimous, and the master of the house is anxious"[122] -- seemingly a completely opposite teaching from the more laid-back adage that follows it!

Way back in my early days as a yeshiva boy in Jerusalem, I asked one of my teachers, the sagely Rav Efrayim Zeitchik about this. He gave me one of his warm grandfatherly smiles, stroked his long grey disheveled beard, wiped the summer sweat from his aging brow, gently whisked away an annoying fly, and said: "Timing and context. It's all about timing and context. There is no contradiction. Life is short, there is a lot to do in our short lifetime, and to do this work is richly rewarding. But alas! We grow lazy, tired, worn down from trying and trying and trying and seeing little or no results. And God is urging us on, reminding us that -- and this is Tar'fon's next sentence in the *Mishnah* -- that the work is not upon us to necessarily complete, but neither are we exempt from the work itself, from the effort, from the endeavor."

Good. Fine. That explains the **Context** part of the equation. What of the **Timing** factor?

"Timing?" he continued, waving at the same fly who

---

[121] *Mishnah, Avo't* 5:22
[122] *Mishnah, Avo't* 2:15

was returning for another shot at his earlobe. "Timing is everything. The Golden Calf, for instance. David and Bathsheba, for instance."

As was his way, he paused and waited, watching me ponder, waiting for me to remember by his clues the teachings of the ancients about how the Golden Calf was not such a horrible thing to create. What was wrong about it was not that we **made** it, but the **urgency** with which we made it. We strayed from the path **hurriedly**, with **urgency**.[123] It was the urgency in building it that spun us into **worshiping** it.[124] Otherwise, it was a meaningful enough sculpture -- meaningful enough that centuries later several of them adorned the sacred sites of the northern kingdom of Israel without incident and absent the wrath of God or of anyone else.[125] Had our ancestors built the Golden Calf like a week or two later, a couple months later, not out of their desperation for a Moses-substitute, it would have been inconsequential[126] and we'd have paid five bucks a head to see it.

As the third-century Shimon bar Chalaf'ta taught: "You set out on a journey, perhaps after the second or third mile you might err in your sense of direction; but certainly not in the **first** mile! Likewise, did Creator say to our ancestors after they hurriedly built the Golden Calf, 'I would have expected you to maybe stray during the second cycle of your wanderings, or the third -- but in the **first**?! *Wow*, man!'"[127]

---

[123] Exodus 32:8 and Deuteronomy 9:16

[124] Exodus 32:8

[125] Second Kings 10:29

[126] *To'rat Hanefesh*, folio 656

[127] *Midrash Sh'mo't Rabbah*, Ch. 32

As for David and Bathsheba, they **indeed** belonged together, just not right then, not in the bubble of time that was born out of David's **urgency**, out of his desperation to have her right then and there. Had he waited, she would have become his wife under more legitimate circumstances. After all, Solomon, who was destined to continue the dynasty and build the Holy Temple, and whose life mission was so divinely ordained that God called him "My son"[128] -- was eventually born of the union of David and Bathsheba, but years **later**, *after* the tragic incident of their illicit affair.[129] Had David waited, had he not acted out of urgency, circumstances would have shifted and Bathsheba would have been unmarried and it would have coincided with the actual time of Solomon's time to arrive on the planet. As the ancients put it: "David and Bathsheba were destined for one another from the time of Creation, but *alas*! David ate **raw** [Rashi: 'He jumped ahead of the destined hour and joined with her illicitly']."[130]

Context and Timing. What a concept.

In the story of David's **later** warfares, it seems he learned his lesson. God advises him not to respond to the charging Philistine army until he is given a sign: the branches of the nearby trees will start to shake. The Philistines charge at the Israelites in full force, yelling, screaming, their spears at the ready, aimed right at the hearts of David's warriors who stand firm under his orders, puzzled as to why David was delaying the order to

---

128 Second Samuel 7:14 and First Chronicles 17:13, 22:10, and 28:26
129 Second Samuel 12:24
130 *Talmud Bav'li, Sanhedrin* 107a

counterattack. They start complaining to David: "What are we waiting for? We can see the whites of their eyes!" And David says "I am instructed by *Elo'heem* not to make a move toward them until I see the branches of the trees begin to shake; and if we attack them before that time, we will surely die. Rather let us die as righteous beings than we die in disobedience to God." In that moment, the branches of the trees began to shake, the Israelites attacked, and the victory was theirs.[131]

These ancient lessons clearly advise us to not jump the gun, to work at being patient with what comes at us, with what we study or experience and cannot in the moment understand -- to wait, to let a little time pass before rendering judgment, before jumping to hurried conclusions, before worrying; to instead live a meaningful life without purpose. In so doing, we may stand a far better chance at achieving that which seems to elude us the most: Clarity.

---

[131] Second Samuel 5:23-25; and *Midrash Yalkot Shimo'nee, Shmu'el Bet*, No. 142

Chapter Twelve

THE SHADOW KNOWS

There is an ancient adage that goes like this: "It is written: 'The life of Man is like a breath exhaling; his days are like a passing shadow'[132] -- meaning, not like the shadow of a wall, nor like the shadow of a tree, but like the shadow of a bird when she is flying."[133] The shadow of a wall or of a tree is temporary, it vanishes with the shifting of sun light. The shadow of a **bird**, however, moves WITH the bird, even as she is in flight.

We are in constant flux. Time shadows us, following our every act, our every movement forward or backward. Time does not simply pass us by, brushing shoulders with us in passing. Time carries us, envelops us, and sweeps us along with it. "We journey with and within time," my teacher the late Rav Efraim Zeitchik used to say. "We ride the waves of time, whether the tides are high or low. In a manner of speaking, we eat time, we drink time; we are shadowed by time."

What a gift it is to take time to **acknowledge** time. To stop for a moment to **receive** the moment, to drink

---

[132] Psalms 144:4
[133] *Midrash Kohelet Rabbah* 81:3

from its wellspring, to connect to it. To realize every now and then that we are in motion, our bodies are aging, our spirits are blossoming, and our feelings are ripening. We are on a journey from and to eternity. We are being carried by a force so clear and real that we are blinded by it and often numb to it. Tapping into it when we can, gifts us with a reminder of the preciousness of our lives, of our mere existence. To **experience** Life, we need to occasionally **feel** it, to stop the world and get off. To know the shadow as well as the shadow knows us.

"How can one know life?" Reb Efraim would ask us. "How can we truly know it when whatever happened is already past, and what is going to happen we don't know yet, and what IS happening we are unconscious of?" The missing link is the moment, he explained, the cognition of time in the present, of the shadow of our wings as we are in flight, in movement, in aliveness. Tapping into the *Now* restores the missing link that bonds past and future. No wonder the narrative of our Torah begins virtually every line with "And." Time is an invitation. In fact, in the Hebrew the word for time and the word for Invitation are actually the same: *z'mahn*.

"For if we are not aware of the present," Rav Zeitchik would say to us, "then surely we will have forgotten yesterday by virtue of not being there anymore, and will then also forget about today by the time tomorrow arrives. And if so, what does one actually get to taste of the flavor of life?"[134] Rather, by being present as much as we can in any given moment, we piece together the fragments of our life, so that our life is not random grains of sand cast

134 *To'rat HaNefesh*, pp. 290-291

into the wind but grains of sand that become integrated enough to forge rich clumps of fertile soil that foster our unfolding.

When we simply **visit** time from time to time, rather than fly **with** it, then our pleasures here are momentary, like the shadow of a tree or of a wall. Here now, gone in an hour or a day. Our moments of delight and inspiration become just that: moments, severed, broken, fragmented, disconnected pieces of some distant detached memory. Then our lives begin to feel like we've only truly **lived** maybe a couple of days in all. Like the ancient mystics put it: "The human can live even a thousand years and still feel like it's been only a single day."[135]

On the other hand, when we live with awareness of each moment, and its connectedness to all other moments past or present, then we thread our lives with so much more joy and mystery and bring cohesiveness as well as nourishment for our spirits even in times of hardship and pain.

The choice remains ours. We can be like a single breath exhaling. Here for a moment, then gone. Or like a traveling shadow, a shadow in movement; the shadow of a bird in flight. Moving from eternity to eternity. Time is more than the mysterious mover of our lives, the elusive "shadow that knows" and follows our every move. Time is the thread. And we are the weavers. And our lives are the fabric waiting to be woven.

---

[135] Zohar, Vol. 1, folio 223b

Chapter Thirteen

SCHNAPPS AND CAKE, OR PEA SOUP?

You know – for the life of me, the most prominent memories I have of Yom Kippur in my more orthodox days are of schnapps and cake. I prayed with the holiest of the holy, the saintliest of saints, and with the most fervor of fervors. Our chanting reached beyond the heavens, bypassed all ten angelic realms and buzzed right past the proverbial Throne of Glory itself. The old master, Reb Eliezer, would abandon his body, his prayer shawl a portal to worlds beyond our own; my classmates transformed before my eyes into ethereal beings as the walls of the yeshiva quaked to the resonating echoes of prayerful voices both loud and whispered, in shouts and in chants, whooshing through the narrow corridors of the Bukharin sector of Jerusalem like the rapids of a river determined to forge new pathways through unforgiving shale.

And yet, most memorable for me was the schnapps and cake served after the fast.

To this day, I swear, I cannot access the sensations of the awesomeness of all those many super-holy Yom Kippurs past, not a single one of them. But every glass of post-Yom Kippur schnapps and every crumb of post-Yom Kippur cake still lingers on my tongue and burns fiercely in the archives of my memory like an Eternal Lamp.

Please allow me to explain something very important.

Everybody loves a good *Kol Nidrei*. We flock to the synagogue on the eve of Yom Kippur specifically to hear someone chant this mournful prayer, basically a rite of nullification, of cancelling any resolutions we may have made or are intent on making. So, while most people celebrate their New Year by **making** resolutions, we celebrate ours by **voiding** them. This is why, on the eve of Yom Kippur, synagogues experience far greater attendance than during any other period, including Yom Kippur day itself. Why? Because we desperately want to hear the *Kol Nidrei* – the Chant of the Nullification of all Resolutions. Don't get me wrong; we are all **for** resolutions, but we are a little leery about their downside.

For example, at a traditional Jewish wedding ceremony we do not have anything remotely resembling "vows." You will never ever hear the word "promise" as in "Do you *promise* to…" And neither will you hear any pronunciation by the rabbi or cantor as in "I now *pronounce* you husband and wife." We don't have any of that in our ceremonies. No commitment, no vows, no promises, and no pronunciations. "Let your 'Yes' be a sincere 'Yes,'" taught the wrongfully-maligned ancient Pharisees, "and your 'No' be a sincere 'No.'"[136] We know what we must do, what it involves, and we will try and do the best we can moment to moment, day by day, but we're not going to contract a life-long walk on eggshells with the shadow of expectations looming

---

[136] *Talmud Bav'li, Baba Bat'ra* 49b

threateningly over us like a thundercloud. Promises are romantic, but they also up the ante when broken. So, we don't promise. We don't make vows. We commit to trying and doing our best moment to moment, day by day, hour by hour. Marriage, we believe, is not about "settling down." It is about "rising up."

Marriage is solidified simply by the public act of two lovers mutually agreeing to jointly do this thing called "marriage," accompanied by the exchange of something of value such as a camel or a ring. The groom gives and the bride accepts. If the groom gives and the bride does not accept, there is no marriage. If the bride gives and the groom accepts, since she derives personal pleasure by his acceptance of her gift it is still as if he gave and she accepted, his gift to her being his acceptance of her gift to him. Without the ingredient of Acceptance, in other words, nothing happens.[137]

It is sort of like a teaching we have that goes like this:

> It is written: "'And you are my witnesses,' sayeth the Lord, 'and I am God.'"[138] Said Shimon bar Yo'chai, "It is as if God is saying 'If you are my witnesses, **then** I am God; if you are **not** my witnesses, then I am **not** God.'"[139]

In the final analysis, our acceptance of God has more weight than God's self-declaration of "I am God."

---

[137] *Talmud Bav'li, Kidushin* 5b
[138] Isaiah 43:12
[139] *Midrash Sif'ri, Pis'ka* 346:3

Likewise, the bride's gesture of acceptance is more powerful than the groom's words of intent. Having the last and final word or act in the negotiation of the marriage, it is the bride who actually **makes** the marriage happen, not the groom. This is the way the ancient teachers set it up in an era and world culture that was almost completely male-dominated. "Ancient Israelite women," observed one noted feminist in the roaring 70's, "fared better than modern western women."[140]

Accepting something from someone is then a far more potent act than **giving** something to someone. Giving is easy. You've got nothing to lose, nothing to feel guilty about. You're scot-free, as they say. Accepting has more power, yes, but it also has more responsibilities. Because, more than the giver, it is the receiver who forges the connection and seals the interaction by the act of acceptance.

It's nice that God gave us existence. But look at all of what that entails on **our** end! Look at all of what you're now strapped with until the day they carry your sorry ass off to Fairlawn. Look at all the responsibilities, the expectations, the struggles involved, the highs and lows, the wear and tear! But yet you accepted what was given and you pay hundreds of thousands to sustain it.

But there are several ways of accepting. One is to simply go along with whatever and passively accept. Another is to actively, consciously, willingly, **deliberately** accept. By choosing the latter, we accept with *chutzpah*! We **choose** life, not by default, not because we happen to **be**, but by conscious choice. We choose, like our ancestor

---

[140] *Religion and Sexism* [Simon and Schuster: 1970], p. 70

Abraham, who **accepted** in spite of the fact that the land God promised him and his descendants had nothing for him to eat or drink upon his initial arrival, forcing him to head down to Egypt for dinner.[141] We choose, in other words, to co-participate in the drama of life, whether we can figure it out or not, and come what may – or may not. In so doing, we reclaim that power so easily lost in the dynamics of acceptance.

Sure enough, comes Yom Kippur Eve and we are reminded not to let the hardships and downsides of acceptance deprecate the sanctity and preciousness of that which we accepted. In the soothing sound of *Kol Nidre*, we are offered relief from the pressures and judgments with which we "acceptees" tend to saddle ourselves. Our guilt over not being able to always come through and live up to what we presume is expected of us in return for the gift of life we accepted, are dissipated by the soothing Song of Nullification, the *Kol Nidre*, which reminds us that "All of the pressures of coming through with what you presume you owe for the life you've been given, for the existence you accept upon yourself daily; all the resolutions you imposed upon yourself or intend to because you think you owe and owe and owe – are hereby nullified. Your debt is forgiven; it never was. You're free to breathe more fully, live more fully, love more fully."

Kol Nidre is then deeper than a ritual for annulling vows, real or imagined. It is a friendly reminder that your existence, your relationship with God or Atom or Intelligent Design -- or what**ever** you want to call that which cannot be named -- is not bound up in vows and

---

[141] Genesis 12:7-19

promises and emotional I.O.U.'s. God **gave** you -- sans expectations. Your credit line is unlimited. God is pleased by your acceptance of the life he gave you, and even more so if and when you can find time and opportunity to actually enjoy some of it.

"In the future," taught Zachariah, a fourth-century spiritual master, "we will have to account before God for all of the pleasures of life we had the desire to enjoy and the opportunity to enjoy [and legally so] – and didn't!"[142]

So, at the conclusion of the Day of Atonement, what would you rather receive? What would feel more comforting for you? This obscure idea called "Atonement"? Or a piece of cake and a *shot* glass?

"Rebbe," I asked in 1967, a tad high on an empty stomach coated in whiskey. "Why always schnapps and cake at the end of the fast? Why not *kugel* and pea soup, for once?"

The old man smiled that ancestral grandfatherly smile of his. "Ay Gershen, Gershen, Gershen. Can't you see what's happening here? You davened all day asking for forgiveness for your sins. Now it's God's turn to respond, and it goes like this: 'Here, have a shot of cognac and a piece of cake.' Now, would you have gotten that kind of reassurance through a bowl of soup?"

You see, *Kol Nidrei* is basically a prelude not to the lengthy Yom Kippur ritual that follows but to the climactic schnapps-and-cake ceremony at the very end. The rest is moot because you've already been absolved before it even began.[143]

---

[142] *Talmud Yerushalmi, Kidushin* [toward the end]

[143] *Talmud Bav'li, Yo'ma* 87b

And it shall come to pass that before they
have even called, I have already answered;
while they are still speaking, I have
already heard.[144]

Life is then about what we do in between *Kol Nidrei* and
schnapps. Life is about what we do in between the moment
we taste the Forbidden Fruit and the moment God asks us
"Where are you?" How we live our lives during this period
will largely determine whether our response will then
be "I heard you coming, so I got nervous because I have
nothing to show for myself"[145] -- or simply: "I am here."[146]
The former response is born out of our search for **purpose**,
as in having to have a reason to exist, a justification; the
latter response is born out of our search for **meaning**, as
in "the fact I exist is justification enough."

Now, don't get me wrong. There is nothing wrong
with purpose itself. Purpose is a good thing. The Tree
of **Knowledge** is a good tree. But it is a good idea to first
spend a little time lounging in the shade of the Tree of **Life**,
which is more about bringing **meaning** to our lives than
purpose. Once we bring meaning to the table, purpose is
eventually served, and in a smorgasbord of varieties, each
determined by its respective meaning. Whatever meaning
you bring to the forefront, in other words, *is* your purpose
in that moment. In this way, purpose is empowered by
meaning rather than the other way around. It is the
difference between a tree that in appearance is robust and

---

[144] Isaiah 65:24

[145] Genesis 3:10

[146] Genesis 22:2

magnificent but its roots are small and short, as opposed to a tree which in appearance seems mediocre but its roots are large and extensive. When a strong wind blows, which of the two do you suppose has the best chance of not wavering and remaining solidly grounded?[147]

Our so-called advanced culture has all but robbed us of the gift of meaning and replaced it with the urgency of purpose. Thus, people rarely ask: "So **tell** me about yourself." Rather, it's mostly: "You got a card?" To paraphrase comedian Jackie Mason: "Everybody is handing out business cards, but the only ones making a living are the printers."

Purpose is competitive. We vie to out-purpose our neighbor, or at the very least achieve an in-kind purpose. In the process, we oftentimes lose sight of what's **really** important and neglect our individual selfhood and its unique possibilities. More and more, people judge us not for who we are but for what we've accomplished, for what sort of justification we've come up with for existing.

This subliminal auto-suggestive need to justify existing stems in turn from a sense of having been put here by no choice of our own. The search for purpose becomes the more urgent when we feel we exist by no choice of our own, because when things get rough there better be sufficient justification for being here that makes going through this shit worthwhile. We are then left with a gaping hole waiting to be filled either by the discovery of some purpose, or by what often turns out to be an addiction of one sort or another.

On the other hand, when we **choose** to exist, we bring

---

[147] *Mishnah, Avot* 3:17

meaning to our lives. There is then no urgent need for figuring out a **reason** to live or some justification to make dealing with life's potpourri of challenges worthwhile. There is no gaping hole begging to be filled because life becomes then not a sentence but a gift of which we are an integral component; a venture in which we are a key partner.

"By our mere existence," taught the 18th-century Tzadok Ha'Kohain, "we perform the sacred Will of Creator who wills us into being and becoming in every moment ....thus, all of our natural functions such as eating, drinking, and lovemaking, all are an integral part of Creator's intent."[148] To bring meaning to our lives does therefore not have to be as arduous a journey as it is cracked up to be. It takes very little effort other than the simple awareness of the **magic** of *being*, coupled with a conscious choice to be an active **participant** in that magic.

Hillel the Elder (1st century B.C.E.) was hurrying down the street one day when several disciples spotted him.

"Master, where are you hurrying to?"

"I am on my way to do God's Will."

"Oh, and what might that be?"

"I'm gonna take a piss."

"Oh? Is that a sacred deed?"

"Yes, for it is part of tending to the well-being of the body."

On another occasion he was seen hurrying through the streets of Jerusalem with a towel on his shoulder. Again, several disciples spotted him.

"Master, where are you hurrying off to?"

---

[148] *Tzid'kat Ha'Tzadik*, No. 173

"I am on my way to do God's Will."

"Oh, and what might it be **this** time?"

"I'm gonna take a bath."

"Oh? Is that a sacred deed?"

"Yes indeed. See how the Romans are cleaning statues of their heroes? And statues are but lifeless **facsimiles** of the human who is created in the Image of God.[149] Shall I then not scrub clean my living flesh, which is **actually** created in the Image of God?"[150]

Now mind you, all this "God" talk is not about "religion." There's not even much about it that is "spiritual." You don't have to be a "believer" to benefit from these ancient wisdoms. They are very simple, universal, and user-friendly, and demand no particular beliefs from you other than the most difficult belief of them all, belief in yourself and in the idea that you are worthy of the entire universe having been created just for you alone.[151] But don't let it go to your head either, lest I remind you of the disappointing fact that the gnat preceded you by eons in the sequence of either Creation or Evolution, whichever you might choose to ascribe to.[152]

"Meaning" means that before I go gallivanting about in search of the Holy Grail of some purported purpose I might presume I have in the scheme of things, I will first bask in the mystery of the scheme of things itself, which is brimming with its **own** purpose. I will dabble and explore with wonder and awe the elusive, and perhaps unfathomable purpose of existence altogether.

---

[149] Genesis 1:27

[150] *Talmud Bav'li, Avot D'Rebbe Natan(nus'cha-bet)*, Ch. 30

[151] *Mishnah, Sanhedrin* 4:5

[152] *Midrash Bereisheet Rabbah* 8:1

In pondering the purpose of existence, the urgency for discovering my own personal purpose shrinks into oblivion, but my sense of meaning becomes further enriched. For I will then realize that in essence I am an integral component of the very purpose I seek; I am – by my mere existence – an essential piece of a far greater purpose than the **micro**cosmic purpose I seek.

Pea soup or cake, friends. Your choice.

Chapter Fourteen

ABEL'S DOG

Are you still with me? Okay, then. Listen.

Cain killed Abel.[153]

This is an important story, and we need to understand what exactly happened between the first two brothers in this ancient narrative of the early history of humanity.

Cain worked the realm of Plant; he was a "worker of the land," the story goes, whereas Abel worked the realm of Animal; he was a "herder of flocks."[154]

Cain would bring Abel the fruit of the earth; and Abel would in turn bring Cain milk and wool from his herds. Thus, the one who worked the realm of Plant benefited from the realm of Animal as well, and the one who worked the realm of Animal benefited from the realm of Plant as well.

So far, so good: The first two brothers are sharing with one another of the respective fruits of their respective labors. All is well.

As Cain worked the earth by the sweat of his brow, he often thought of how it was his very hard work that

---

[153] Genesis 4:8

[154] Genesis 4:2

enabled Abel to raise his herds. If not for the oats and alfalfa which Cain had seeded and irrigated -- and otherwise managed and worried about day and night, season after season -- Abel would not have had the luxury of peacefully daydreaming in the fields while his flocks peacefully grazed and nibbled. Secondly, it took a lot more time and effort and energy and struggle for Cain to plant, grow and gift Abel with a head of lettuce than it did for Abel to gift Cain with a slice of cheese. Thirdly, Abel's twin sister, who was also his wife (since there were no other people, yet[155]) was far more beautiful and fun to hang with than **Cain's** twin sister/wife. So, Cain began to resent the fact that his brother had ended up with the better end of the deal all across the board.

After a number of days and nights of brooding and brewing and stewing with all of this, Cain decided to pay a visit to his father, Adam.

"My dear son," Adam began. "What might be helpful to you is the practice of sacrifice."

"What is *sacrifice*?"

"Sacrifice is the act of acknowledging that in essence nothing is really ours, for all belongs to Creator, and we are but guests sojourning in the Land of the Living. You see, in letting **go** of what we own, we free ourselves of *being* owned."

Cain then realized that his pain over the inequality and unfairness in his life was rooted in his obsession with **po**ssession, with what his brother had that he didn't, and with what *he* had but which benefited Abel more than it did *him*, such as the pastures which Abel used

---

[155] *Talmud Bav'li, Yevamot* 62a

for his herds at the expense of Cain's hard work. And the antidote to his discontentment, his father now advised, was sacrifice. And so he designed and constructed an altar, took of the fruits of his fields, and offered them to Creator as an acknowledgment that in essence all that he possessed or **wished** to possess belonged neither to him nor to his hard work but to Creator who gifted him with mind, spirit and body, and with the wherewithal to follow his passion of working the soil and conjuring fruition out of possibility.

When Cain had finished offering his sacrifice, Abel appeared with his weekly supply of milk and cheese and asked Cain what he was doing. Cain showed Abel his altar and told him about his meeting with their father. He explained to his brother how he was sacrificing some of his produce to Creator, and how it felt liberating to do so, to let go of his obsession with attachments to ownership. Abel was impressed and thought the idea was brilliant.

Finally, Cain was at peace and began focusing on appreciating what he **had** rather than on what he did *not* have. He loved his work more. He loved his wife more. He loved his handiwork, especially the beautiful altar he had designed and built…but upon which his sacrifice continued to linger, day after day, appearing to not be received by Creator and instead beginning to reek as it began to rot.

Hmmm.

Trying not to think about it too much, Cain grabbed a variety of vegetables and headed toward Abel's place to bring his brother his weekly supply of fresh produce and maybe pick up some cheese and butter. As he drew near to Abel's place, he stopped dead in his tracks, stunned by what he saw. Lo and behold – there was Abel standing in front of what appeared to be an altar, and upon which lay the remains of a sheep slowly sizzling in a huge flame whose smoke rose high above the earth. And before Cain's very eyes, a second fire appeared from out of the heavens, enveloped the entire altar and consumed what turned out to be **Abel's** sacrifice – *poof*! Gone. It seemed Creator had received Abel's copycat offering, while Cain's trademarked cabbage continued to decompose on *his* altar!

Cain was in shock. He approached his brother: "What did you do to that sheep?"

"I released its spirit. I let its blood pour out, and as it did so, its life force departed. Did father not explain to you how the ritual of sacrifice is performed?"

"I didn't ask. I figured I'd just place some produce on the special altar I built, and offer it to Creator."

"Understood, Cain, but for me it's different. Were I to place a couple of sheep on the altar, they would hop right off. That is why I had to do it this way, and it worked! You saw yourself how a fire descended from the heavens and consumed my sacrifice, as no doubt occurred for *your* sacrifice."

"Actually, it didn't occur at all. My sacrifice continues to sit on the altar untouched except by flies and ants."

"Perhaps, brother, perhaps it's different with vegetation. After all, how do you release the life-force of a yam?"

"Not funny."

Cain left his gifts with his brother and departed in a

huff. Arriving home, he sat himself down on the ground beside his altar, brooding, when Creator spoke to him.

"Cain, why are you so upset? Your face is barely recognizable. Did you slip-slide back to Square-One? Just days ago, you acknowledged to me that you appreciated what you had, and that it all belongs to and comes from me…bla bla bla…yakity yakity yak…and now *this*?"

"You accepted my brother's offering and not mine. I offered **my** sacrifice *first*; he got the idea from *me*! Why did you not accept *mine*?"

"Listen to yourself. Have you truly let *go* of attachments, or did you simply shift from attachment-to-possessiveness to attachment-to-expectations, particularly in regard to **me**? I have no need or any use for either plant *or* animal, Cain. I created both. Your brother's sacrifice reflected his capacity to truly let go, to truly sacrifice, for he gave not merely *of* his flocks, but of the *choicest* of his flocks.[156] All that aside, Cain, a far greater sacrifice for me would be if you could sacrifice your attachment to the ritual of sacrifice altogether, an attachment that now has you fuming. If you sincerely want to make the change you were originally trying to make in your life, you still can, but if you were just trying to conceal your Shadow Self in the guise of self-righteous piety, let me forewarn you that your Shadow Self is scratching fiercely at the door, eager to free-up the very impulses you have so sanctimoniously swept under the rug."[157]

Creator's counsel was nice and wise as always, Cain thought to himself, but what could the immortal **Creator**

---

[156] Genesis 4:4
[157] Genesis 4:6-7

possibly know of downhome mortal anguish? And so, hard as he tried not to, he ended up seething and fuming all night long.

By morning, Cain was on his way back to Abel's place, murmuring and ranting as he approached. He had had enough of all this…giving so much, doing so much, expending so much, with nothing but frustration and disappointment in return, while his brother was happily prancing about without a worry in the world. "Abel!" Cain called to his brother. "Would you concede that my strong point is stewardship of the land, and your is animal husbandry?"

"I guess."

"Good, so let's divide the planet equally. You maintain jurisdiction over the animals, and I over the land. Agreed?"

"Sure, brother, whatever makes you happy."

"Fine, then. Now, get your filthy animals off my land!"

"*What*?! Have you gone stark-raving *mad*? Where will I *take* them?"

"That's *your* problem! The land is *mine*, so get them off *now*!"

And so, wherever Abel led his flocks and herds, Cain followed him and drove him away. "The land is mine, remember?" he would shout at Abel. "Away with your herds!"

Finally, Abel had had just about all he could take of his brother's shenanigans and refused to move any further. The two got into a shoving fight during which Cain tripped over a rock and fell backward onto the earth. Abel turned around and began walking back toward his herd. Cain was furious. There remained only one way, he now thought, of freeing himself from the angst which was consuming him in regard to his brother: *relieve his brother of **his** life-force as his brother had done to the sheep on the altar*! "And so, Cain rose toward Abel his brother and killed him"[158] with the very rock over which he had tripped, and watched his brother drop to the earth as the life-force bled from his head. Cain quickly hid his brother's lifeless body by covering it with some earth and leaves, and headed home feeling finally liberated from his unhealthy entanglement with Abel. In a day or so, Abel's wife would surely be his, as would **all** that Abel had, including his peace of mind, that sense of tranquility he had coveted for years.

Returning home, Cain went straightaway to his altar and knocked his rotting sacrifice off the slab, when Creator spoke to him.

"Where is Abel your brother?"

"Master of the Universe!" replied Cain. "You assigned me to watch over field and orchard, not over my brother."

"Have you taken your brother's life from him, as well as all that was his?"

"What makes you assume such a horrible thing about me?"

"The sound of the bloods of your brother, they are crying out to me."[159]

"Bloods?"

"Yes, many bloods. Countless bloods. For you have destroyed not only your brother but all of the many generations that could have emerged from him."

---

[158] Genesis 4:8

[159] Genesis 4:10

In that moment, Cain was overcome by intense dread. He had done away with far more than a single person; he'd destroyed an entire world.[160] The anguish he now felt was far more severe than what he'd been dealing with when his brother was alive

"My error is too great for me to bear!" he now cried.

"Indeed, it is so. Moreover, you have also destroyed your chances for the very peace of mind you had hoped for. Even your passion for working the earth will never be the same, for you have abused your relationship with her by using her to conceal the blood of your brother. And the animals of the field, who enjoyed a special relationship with your brother, they will abandon you, if not seek your harm, for you have deprived them of their Keeper. You have essentially isolated yourself and placed yourself in a situation that leaves you restless and wandering."

"How will I survive all this? All of Creation now despises me and will seek to take my life!"

Creator then summoned the *tav*, the last of the twenty-two conjures by which the universe was created,[161] and sealed the *tav* upon Cain's forehead on the very same spot of his forehead where Cain had struck his brother with the rock, and assured Cain of its protection. Creator also summoned Abel's dog, the dog which used to watch over the well-being of Abel's flocks, and assigned it to accompany Cain on his wanderings and protect him from any creature who would seek his harm. And so, Cain walked off into the sunset, with Abel's dog at his heel.

A short time later, Adam and Eve uncovered Abel's

---

[160] *Mishnah, Sanhedrin* 45

[161] Namely, the twenty-two letters of the Hebrew alphabet

body and went into mourning. They also felt at a loss as to what to do with the corpse of their son since, prior to Abel, no human had ever died. As they sat weeping and grieving, a raven landed in front of them clutching the lifeless body of one of its own in its talons. The raven lay it gently upon the earth and began burying it in the earth. Said Adam: "As the raven is doing, so shall we," and they buried Abel in the earth. Creator was pleased that the raven deliberately buried its kin in front of Adam and Eve with the intention of demonstrating what was to be done to a corpse. In return, Creator pledged that whenever the raven calls for rain, Creator would respond to their call and bring the rain, as is written: "Who gives to Animal her sustenance; onto the offspring of Raven when they call."[162]

And now you know why Creator later instructed the Israelites to refrain from donning garments woven of a blend of wool and linen.[163] For wool is from the realm of Animal, whose Keeper was Abel, and linen is from the realm of Plant, whose Keeper was Cain. Each realm had its very own distinct "Day" in the Genesis of Creation, and each ought to be respected for the uniqueness of its realm, and neither should rival with the other, for while all are One, all are not the same. Said Yehoshua ben Kor'cha (second century): "Thus did Creator declare, 'The respective sacrifices of Cain and Abel (plant and animal) shall forever not become intermingled.'"[164]

And now you also know why every one of the Five

---

[162] Psalms 147:9

[163] Deuteronomy 22:11

[164] *Midrash Pirkei D'Rebbe Eliezer*, Chapter 21

Commandments on the second tablet of the Decalogue, having to do with interpersonal relations, begins with the "Mark of Cain," the *Tav*, as in:

> You shall not --
> murder (T*ir'tzach*)
> abuse sexually (T*in'af*)
> steal (T*ig'nov*)
> testify falsely (T*a'aneh*)
> crave what others have (T*ach'mo'd*)[165]

And now you also *also* know why the ancient biblical injunction against wearing a garment woven of wool and linen appears immediately following the commandment to "Love your neighbor as yourself."[166]

In the course of our natural longing for purpose, we often end up sacrificing meaning. For example, at the very same time the ancient Israelites were instructed to build a special sanctuary intended as sort of an earthly "guest room" for God, they were also instructed not to overwork their donkeys and oxen in the process.[167] Moreover, they were reminded that it was still important to step back from their sense of empowerment as creators to remember that they are creat**ed**.[168] In other words, lest they lose themselves in the zeal of **purpose** – however sacred -- they were reminded of the importance of **meaning**. And that meaning overrides purpose.

The way in which these ancient instructions were laid

---

[165] Exodus 20:13-17
[166] Leviticus 19:18 and 19
[167] Deuteronomy 5:14 and 25:4; Exodus 8:10 and 23:12
[168] Exodus 31:13

out took into consideration the fact that in our search for purpose, we often overlook meaning. In our endeavors to "**become** someone" we tend to overlook who we already **are**. The more we focus our sights on achieving **purpose**, the more we blur our sights on achieving **meaning**.

Yes, please hurry and get that log over to the sanctuary construction site. But don't yoke an ox and a donkey together to do so.[169] Else, you're all about purpose and zero about meaning. Becoming conscientious about the different needs and paces of varying species of the creatures with whom you share this planet, is meaningful. And it overrides the purpose of building a symbolic sanctuary for "housing" the Divine Presence.

I've met so many people in my long life who were so sorely driven to purpose that they'd but lost all sense of meaning. They would teach, lecture, write bestselling books and be so full of purpose that one wondered if they were actually mortal. Ironically, people would never refer to them in relation to their purpose, only to their "success." They were "successful." They had succeeded in selling books, becoming famous, and lecturing around the world, but for what purpose? Was it to change the world? Well, folks, I haven't seen any changes yet for the better in spite of all the bestsellers on how to improve our lives and in spite of the millions who flock regularly to hear the preaching of the so-called Good Word.

The purpose we **seek**, you see, is personal and therefore small, a tiny grain of sand amid a beach-full. It **looks** big on people who are acclaimed as "successful" only because

---

[169] Deuteronomy 22:10

they managed to possess a bigger clump of those teeny-tiny grains than most of us.

You see, **Purpose** comes in two basic flavors: Purpose we ourselves design and strive for, and Purpose we are given.

The purpose we are **given** is cosmic, a single star amid a universe-full, albeit gargantuan enough to contain hundreds of earths plus a moon or two. And for purpose to be **given**, one needs to create space for it to be received, and one does so by focusing on **meaning**; one does so not by looking for reasons and justifications but by stepping to the plate to do what needs to be done in the moment that it is called for. To paraphrase Hillel the Elder (1st century, B.C.E.): "In a situation in which no one is doing what needs to be done, **you** do it!"

Smiling at a co-worker you pass by is meaningful. Keeping an extra buck in your pocket in case you encounter a panhandler, is meaningful. Going out of your personal preference-zone to ask your love or your kid if he or she wants a sandwich, is meaningful. Justifications, reasons, purpose – they all get in the way of so much of what we ought to just be doing because we **can**; because it makes life's precious moments the more precious, the more meaningful. Purpose won't improve the world. Meaning will. The focus on purpose **hinders**. The focus on meaning **inspires**.

Yitzchak Eichenthal isn't famous. I knew him way back when he and his wife B'racha and their 14 or more children lived in an old run-down house in Brooklyn, New York. Yitzchak was an accountant. Never wrote a book in his life. Never gave a lecture to more than maybe a handful of people in the local basement synagogue. I never got the sense in all my many years of knowing this man and his wife that they were looking for **purpose** in their lives. But one thing I **can** tell you. They sure had an awful lot of **meaning**. Their house was always filled, not only with their own kids but with wayward teens, wandering grown-ups, out-of-town travelers. If you needed help with anything, you called Yitzchak or B'racha Eichenthal, a very busy couple who were too busy with living a meaningful life to be bothered with purpose. And in their focus on meaningfulness, they created ample space over the years for purpose to be gifted to them, not the small kind of purpose of the personal sort but the enormous purpose of the cosmic sort. They had no need to go **looking** for purpose. It came to them spontaneously in response to the **meaning** that **they** brought.

You see, Cain found the rite of sacrificing **purposeful**. Abel found it **meaningful**. One person might sacrifice for the purpose of placating or winning the favor of God, while another might sacrifice as a way of expressing meaningfulness, such as gratitude and acknowledgment. In his preoccupation with the **purpose** of sacrifice – presumed to be the act of God accepting his gift – Cain overlooked the far more meaningful drama of the gift which God was giving **him** by engaging him in a one-on-one discussion about his personal internal struggles!

Some seventeen hundred years ago, a major fire broke out in the neighborhood of the saintly master Rav Huna. Miraculously, though, not a single home on Rav Huna's street was so much as tinged, let alone singed, by the shooting flames, and of course everyone on that street thanked the day they decided to live on the street of this famous wonder-worker.

That night, however, all the folks on Rav Huna's block experienced the unusual phenomenon of a collective dream. And in that dream they were told that their homes were spared not at **all** in the merit of the saintly Rav Huna but in the merit of some little old lady down the street who always kept her oven warm and at the ready on the eve of every Sabbath, inviting anyone who needed to use it to come on down and do their baking in her home.[170]

Okay. I know. You're waiting to read more about Abel's *dog*. Wasn't Abel's dog supposedly the point of this entire chapter? And yet he is only mentioned in passing?

Let me tell you about Abel's dog and his relationship to all of this, and how Abel's dog teaches us about living a meaningful life.

You know how loyal dogs are toward their human partners. In Hebrew, for example, "dog" is "*kelev*" a word which, when split in two, reads "*kol lev*," literally: "All Heart."

Now, can you so much as **imagine** what Abel's dog had to overcome when he was assigned to escort Cain after having witnessed his beloved Abel being **killed** by Cain? And, on top of that, being asked by Creator to **protect** Cain? I mean, could God not have asked some **other** mutt to do the job?

Abel's dog, you see, was able to deal with the challenge of his assignment because he distinguished between self-implied purpose and cosmic-gifted purpose. Self-implied

---

[170] *Talmud Bav'li, Ta'anit* 21b

purpose dictated that his purpose as Abel's dog was to look after Abel and **only** Abel. Cosmic-gifted purpose dictated that his purpose as a carrier of the breath and intent of Creator was to accept the invitation of the moment and rise to the occasion no matter the subject or the circumstance. After all, he had been partnered with a man who in his lifetime lived not with his focus on purpose but on meaning. Abel didn't bring Creator the purpose-driven gift of a sacrifice as did his brother Cain, but a gift infused with meaning: "And Cain brought from the fruit of the ground an offering onto Infinite-All. And as for Abel, he too brought, but from the *firstborn* of his flock."[171]

Firstborn is an important distinction. It is meaningful. Purpose says, "Bring God an offering," like some kind of bribe in a way, so that God will make sure the rains continue and the cabbage grows. There is an end-objective. Meaning says, "If I am going to bring God an offering, let it not be some token gift but a meaningful acknowledgment that everything I've achieved, especially my first novel, my first child, the first calf of my herd, my very first debut at anything I've done – all of it was enabled by the Creator's benevolence." Because, face it: when it comes to "first," we are so much more inclined to claim it for ourselves than we would for "second" or "third." In other words, it is far simpler to thank God for your second accomplishment than for your first. We take hundreds of hours of videos of our firstborn, maybe fifty for our **second** child, a measly dozen for our **third**, and, at best, maybe scribble a caricature for our fourth.

---

[171] Genesis 3:3-4

If I am purpose-oriented, then "First" is about **me** and **my** achievement, **my** success, and I am moved to declare: "My might and the power of my own hands has achieved all of this!"[172] It's about **my** purpose. When we are purpose-oriented, our existential question about life is: "What's in it for **me**?" When we are **meaning**-oriented, our existential question about life is: "Did you eat yet?"

Abel's dog accepts an opportunity of meaning over that of purpose. And in so doing, he is **given** purpose, a purpose far more meaningful than any he himself could have come up with. By letting **go** of purpose, he **achieves** purpose, and he does so through an act that is meaningful, namely the task of accompanying Cain on his lonesome wanderings without so much as a bark of protest. The presence of Abel's dog at his heel will now serve Cain as a constant reminder of his brother and what he did to him. And Abel's dog, in choosing to accompany his partner's killer, will remind Cain that it's not all about either of them – that there is a far bigger picture to be reckoned with, of which both are an important and integral part, and which comes to life when we bring meaning to it.

Abel's dog does not yelp at Creator's assignment, arguing that to accompany Cain does not suit his purpose, as if his purpose had been about Abel. Abel's dog accepts the invitation of the moment at **hand** rather than dilly-dally around the moment that **passed**. Abel's dog was into meaningfulness, and understood that every moment has its own so-called purpose if only we would bring meaning to it.

In our everyday lives we are accorded opportunities

---

[172] Deuteronomy 8:17

to make our existence meaningful, from the opportunity to smile at someone who looks sullen, or relieve a total stranger of extra stress in their lives by not tailgating them on the roadway, or taking a few seconds to admire and appreciate a beautiful tree or flower or sunset or the fact that your cancer is in remission or that your head hurts but your teeth don't. The opportunities are countless and everywhere and every moment.

Sadly, what gets in our way of discovering meaning in even the small steps we take along our life walk are our regrets and other forms of self-deprecation that is awakened when we get too close to an opportunity for meaningfulness. After all, who am I to be this saint who is going to inspire a smile on so-and-so's somber face? After what *I've* done this morning? Forget it. I am not worthy of doing anything meaningful in light of my bad. In fact, it makes me uncomfortable to so much as imagine doing anything meaningful as dark as I feel. I ain't no hypocrite, you know. I know what I did yesterday, and if I do something meaningful right now it will be like an outright denial of the wrong I committed last night. So, no way. I'm gonna walk right by this opportunity and any other that might come my way.

You know, the 18th-century wisdom teacher, Yisra'el Ba'al Shem, used to say that worse than sinning is believing you're a sinner.

So the next time you look back, instead of seeing your past wrongdoings following at your heels, see Abel's dog. And then go fetch some meaning.

Meaningfulness. Don't leave home without it.

Chapter Fifteen

THE JEWEL

We are all looking for the elusive "Jewel," that one un-identifiable thing that would gift us with deep inner joy and purpose, and give us the answer to all of our questions, not to mention the meaning of life altogether. This jewel, the ancients tell us, only **appears** to elude you, to exist far outside of you, requiring you to travel long distances and through great struggles to discover it. In reality, however, it is not outside of you, but buried deep within your core self like a seed waiting to be conjured to fruition.[173]

Once upon a time, there lived a great master named Yudan of Hodu. Hodu is Hebrew for "India," by the way. Yudan earned his livelihood as a fisherman and went out to sea on lengthy voyages solo, returning to his home only after weeks of trawling way out in the middle of the ocean. For provisions on such lengthy voyages, he stored hundreds of dried-up salted birds on the boat, sort of like bird-jerky. (Not to worry – no animals were hurt in the making of this story either.)

One stormy day, as he was out on deck hoisting a sail, Yudan noticed something shining in the waters deep

---

[173] Deuteronomy 30:12

below. It was **the** jewel, the one we just spoke of. It was everything he'd always been searching and hoping for, encrypted within a brilliant gem at the bottom of the sea. He had finally discovered the meaning of life, the answer to all questions, the ultimate joy of being and becoming, his ultimate purpose in life -- and all he had to do was dive in and seize it.

And so he did. Into the raging sea he dove, head first, and, reaching the bottom, he was about to grab hold of the jewel when a giant sea-dragon appeared as if from out of nowhere and snatched the jewel from right under him and swam away. Frustrated, Yudan watched the jewel disappear from sight when suddenly a giant raven dove into the waters, bit off the head of the giant sea-dragon, thereby freeing the jewel from its jaws.

Seeing his opportunity to retrieve the jewel, Yudan swam hurriedly toward the sinking jewel when suddenly a **second** sea-dragon appeared as if from out of nowhere, snatched the jewel from Yudan's reach, and dropped it deliberately on the severed body of the first sea-dragon who instantaneously grew a brand-new head, became resurrected, grabbed the jewel, and swam away with its partner.

Yudan was now twice as frustrated, not only because he had almost had the jewel in his grasp twice and **lost** it twice, but even more so now that he had witnessed the magical powers of the jewel, particularly its ability to restore the dead to life!

He was about to give up and swim back to his boat when he noticed the giant raven returning to the scene, then swooping down upon the two sea-dragons. A massive struggle ensued, creating tsunami-like waves, throwing Yudan back and forth, up and down, preventing him from reaching the boat. As he struggled to keep his head above the hammering waves, he saw the raven fly up into the sky, the jewel firmly held in its talons, and then drop it onto the deck of the boat.

Yudan was elated. His joy gave him the strength and stamina to swim against the torrential waves and climb back onto his boat. Once on board, he reached for the jewel again, but the waves, still choppy and tempestuous from the battle of the giant creatures, rocked his boat so that the jewel rolled away from him and continued rolling down the deck to where he stored the salted birds. As soon as it hit the salted birds, they of course became alive and quickly flew off – taking the jewel with them.

And so, Yudan was left on the now-bare deck of his boat, totally alone, absent any provisions, absent the jewel in which was encrypted everything he had ever longed for and looked for, left only with himself and nothing else.

"I almost had it!" he cried aloud, turning to the heavens. "I almost had it **three times**!!"

"No," came a whisper in the wind. "No, Yudan, you never had it until **now**."

'Until **now**?!" Yudan asked, realizing it was the voice of the Great Mystery out of which all comes into being and becoming. "But now I am left with **nothing**, not what I wanted to have and not what I already had all along and not what I've been searching for all my life! I am left with nothing but **myself**!"

"Exactly," the voice replied. "The Jewel of All is not outside of you. It is deep within you. And when you purport to seek it beyond yourself, it will elude you and draw you into chaos and frustration. It is neither in the heavens above nor in the earth below, nor in the waters beneath the earth, but in your heart of hearts, waiting to be awakened, and on your lips, waiting to be spoken.[174] You **are** the very jewel you seek."

Exactly. And it waits patiently for you to polish it and make it shine like never before.

One day, some three hundred years ago, a great master teacher known as Bunim was strolling through the woods when he encountered one of his disciples sitting on a rock, weeping.

"My son," said the master, "why are you crying?"

"My dear teacher, I am so frustrated. Here I am, a living being, all of whose limbs and organs are in perfect order and all of whose senses are functioning in good health. And yet, I cannot for the life of me figure out what my purpose is! I cannot figure out what it is I was created for and what I am good for in this life!"

"My son," said the master, "those are the exact same questions *I've* been carrying with me my entire life **too**!"

"So, what should we **do**, Master?"

Bunim took his disciple by the arm and helped him up from off the rock and said:

"What should we **do**? We should go and get something to **eat**."

Bon Appetit!

---

[174] Deuteronomy 30:11-14

Printed in the United States
By Bookmasters